HIGH POWER
AUDIO AMPLIFIER CONSTRUCTION

Other Titles of Interest

HIGH POWER
AUDIO AMPLIFIER CONSTRUCTION

by

R. A. Penfold

BERNARD BABANI (publishing) LTD
THE GRAMPIANS
SHEPHERDS BUSH ROAD
LONDON W6 7NF
ENGLAND

Please Note

© 1991 BERNARD BABANI (publishing) LTD

First Published – April 1991
Reprinted – March 1995
Reprinted – July 1998

British Library Cataloguing in Publication Data
Penfold, R. A.
    High power audio amplifier construction.
    1. Amplifiers
    I. Title
    621.3893

    ISBN 0 85934 222 0

Cover Design by Gregor Arthur
Printed and bound in Great Britain by Cox & Wyman Ltd, Reading

Preface

For most domestic purposes, amplifiers having output powers of about 50 watts r.m.s. per channel or less are perfectly adequate. However, there are some applications, particularly P.A. (public address) applications, that require substantially higher output powers. Really high output powers of about 500 watts r.m.s. or more are difficult to achieve using standard "off the shelf" components from ordinary electronic component retailers. The same is not true for output powers of around 400 watts r.m.s. or less, which can now be achieved without having to resort to any exotic and difficult (or impossible) to obtain components. Output powers of this order are adequate for most purposes, and higher powers can effectively be achieved by using multiple loudspeaker arrays with a separate power amplifier driving each loudspeaker.

This book provides relatively simple designs which offer good performance and maximum output powers of around 50 to 400 watts r.m.s. Note that these are true continuous r.m.s. figures per amplifier, and are not some form of "total music power" or other rather misleading form of power rating. These amplifiers will provide high output powers indefinitely, and not just for a few output cycles at a fairly high frequency, or on single pulses! This point should be borne in mind when comparing the power ratings of these designs with those of other amplifiers.

Background information and some theory is provided in the first two chapters. The third chapter provides some practical circuits for amplifiers using power MOSFETs and high power bipolar transistors in the output stages. Suitable mains power supply circuits are included. Printed circuit board designs are provided for the power MOSFET amplifiers, and wiring diagrams for the power supplies are included. Constructing these units is not particularly difficult, and is a task which is probably not beyond the capabilities of anyone with a certain amount of experience at electronic project construction. However, as high power audio circuits inevitably involve the use of quite high supply voltages and currents, I could not recommend these projects for anyone with limited experience of project construction. Minor errors could cause a lot of costly damage, and could even be dangerous. No constructional information is provided for the amplifiers based on bipolar output transistors. These are really only included for those with considerable electronics experience — the power MOSFET designs offer much easier alternatives for those of more limited experience.

R. A. Penfold

Contents

Chapter 1

HIGH POWER PROBLEMS

For most audio power amplifier applications modern technology provides solutions in the form of suitable integrated circuits. Despite improvements over the years though, there are no readily available integrated circuits capable of providing really high output powers. It would be as well here to define what we mean by "high power", since there is no rigid dividing line between medium and high power levels. Defining this term is very much a "how long is a piece of string" type problem. Most audio power amplifiers, for hi-fi, guitar use, etc., seem to have output powers of about 45 watts r.m.s. or less. In this book we will take "high power" to mean anything above this level, or about 50 watts r.m.s. or more in other words.

I suppose that we should also put an upper limit on things as well, since above a certain power level we are really into the realms of what would be more accurately termed "ultra-high power". In this book we will only be dealing with amplifiers having output powers of up to about 300 watts r.m.s. Going above this power level generally requires unusual techniques and circuits based on some highly specialised components.

These specialised components are difficult or impossible for the home constructor to obtain. Improvisation might provide a solution, but it might also lead to a lot of wasted time, effort, and money. High power audio amplifiers are within the capability of anyone who has a certain amount of experience at electronics construction. Ultra-high power designs are a more difficult prospect. It would be very easy to end up with something that failed to work, or worse still, which worked for a while and then (perhaps literally) went up in a puff of smoke!

Warnings
It is only fair to point out that even with the high power designs described here, mistakes could easily prove costly. The voltages and currents involved are inevitably quite high.

1

A mistake which sends a massive amount of power to the wrong part of a circuit will inevitably cause a spectacular failure. Get things wrong and you could easily have the transistors and electrolytic capacitors in the circuit literally exploding. There is not just the cost of replacement parts to worry about — there is also the safety aspect to consider.

Any audio power amplifier having an output power of a few watts or more tends to be operated close to the point at which it self-destructs due to overheating, excessive current flows, or whatever. High power designs almost invariably have to take components very close indeed to their maximum ratings. Even given that manufacturers normally play safe on most ratings, leaving generous margins above the published figures, trying to take the designs featured in this book beyond their specified power ratings is not a good idea. It could easily lead to the immediate failure of the equipment, and even if the equipment should survive in the short term, its medium to long term reliability would probably not be very good. You have been warned!

To avoid costly errors, check and double check everything before connecting one of these amplifier circuits to a power supply. Although many electronic project constructors operate a policy of connecting things up and switching them on first, followed by checking only if problems arise, this is definitely not an acceptable practice in the current context. You might have destroyed every semiconductor in the circuit by the time you get around to checking for errors! Check everything thoroughly first — switch on and try out the amplifiers second.

Ideally, when the circuits are initially tested they should be powered from a lower than normal supply voltage. A bench power supply having built-in current limiting is probably the best power source for this initial testing. Apart from being able to provide a lower and safer supply voltage, the current limiting will protect the circuit against drawing really high power levels. This should ensure that there are no "zapped" semiconductors if there is a fault of some kind in the circuit. If no suitable power supply is available, perhaps the mains transformer in the amplifier's normal power supply will have one or more tappings that will enable it to provide a reduced voltage for testing purposes.

Do not omit any fuses that are shown in the circuits featured in this book (or any other publication come to that). Fuses have their limitations, the main one being that they are relatively slow in operation. Even the so-called "quick-blow" variety are not particularly fast by electronic standards. A severe overload may well take almost a second to "blow" the fuse. Semiconductor current limiting circuits operate in a matter of microseconds, and will usually prevent any damage to the semiconductors in the main circuit. Fuses are not fast enough to provide the same degree of protection. Fuses also tend to ignore minor overloads. They might eventually blow, but perhaps only after the overload has been present for several minutes or more. Semiconductor current limiting and overload cutout circuits have well defined trigger levels.

Despite these problems, fuses are in some respects the more practical choice. They are cheap, simple, and produce minimal power losses. Semiconductor protection circuits need not be particularly complex, but they are quite expensive where high power levels are involved, and they tend to produce quite significant power losses. In most cases fuses will prevent any serious damage to components not already damaged when a fault condition occurs, and they should always be sufficient to prevent problems such as components overheating or wiring burning out when a serious fault occurs.

Treat the output signal of a high power amplifier with due respect. Short circuits on the output can cause massive currents to flow. Apart from the likelihood of damage to the output transistors of the amplifier, pretty massive currents can flow in the output wiring if the output is short circuited while the amplifier is being driven hard. The currents might even be high enough to melt wiring, or to cause the plastic insulation to burn. Always use good quality cables and connectors of adequate rating for the job. Figure of eight type "bell" cable might be fine for low power music centres, etc., but it is inadequate for high power amplifiers. You could easily end up with more power being lost in the cable than reaches the loudspeaker, possibly with dire consequences for the cable. Use proper heavy duty loudspeaker cable, and avoid temporary lash-ups that are unreliable. These could prove to be costly or even dangerous.

Some audio enthusiasts apparently use a system of placing the two bare output leads in their mouth in order to determine whether or not a signal is coming down the cable correctly. This simple test procedure will normally produce a strong tingling sensation if all is well. With a high power amplifier it would probably result in a trip to the nearest casualty unit for treatment! Remember that with high power amplifiers there can be well over one hundred volts peak to peak coming down the loudspeaker cable, not the few volts peak to peak associated with low to medium power amplifiers.

Loudspeaker Matching

Transistors are essentially low voltage devices. Most types will only operate reliably at potentials of about 30 volts or less. Special types can operate at much higher voltages than these, and for high power audio use it is necessary to resort to these high voltage devices. For a given loudspeaker impedance, the higher the output power required, the higher the drive voltage must be. For a standard 8 ohm impedance loudspeaker, the required drive voltage becomes surprisingly large at high powers. This table lists some output powers, together with the approximate r.m.s. and peak to peak drive voltages required for each one.

Output Power	V_{RMS}	$V_{p\text{-}p}$
1 watt	2.82V	8V
5 watts	6.32V	17.83V
10 watts	8.94V	25.22V
50 watts	20V	56.6V
100 watts	28.28V	80V
300 watts	48.98V	138.15V
500 watts	63.2V	178.7V

At 10 watts r.m.s. the peak to peak drive voltage is quite reasonable at only about 25 volts. Most transistors, especially power types, are capable of handling voltages of this order. At 50 watts r.m.s. matters are more difficult, with a peak to peak drive level of about 56 volts needed. There are relatively few linear semiconductors that will operate reliably at voltages as high as this, and at higher powers the situation gets steadily worse. Something not too far short of 200 volts peak to peak is needed in order to give 500 watts r.m.s. into an 8-ohm impedance loudspeaker.

The situation is actually somewhat worse than these figures would suggest. No transistor output stage is capable of producing a peak to peak output voltage that is equal to the supply voltage. The efficiency in this respect varies substantially from one design to another, but at the high currents involved in this application, the voltage drops across power transistors are generally quite high. With bipolar transistors the discrepancy between the supply voltage and the peak to peak output potential could easily be 10% or more. Losses are generally higher with power f.e.t. devices, which tend to have higher minimum "on" resistances than would be ideal. With these it is not uncommon to have a peak to peak output level that is around 20% less than the supply voltage.

Another factor to bear in mind is that most high power audio amplifiers are not fed from stabilised power supplies. Ideally I suppose they would be, but in practice there is the high cost of the stabiliser circuit to consider. As yet, inexpensive monolithic voltage regulators are not capable of handling the kinds of supply voltages and currents involved in high power audio applications. Also, a stabilised supply results in a certain amount of wasted power, which has to be compensated for by using a higher voltage mains transformer. In addition to the extra cost, this also gives increased size and weight. Although a stabilised supply has potential advantages, these are normally outweighed by the increased cost, bulk, and complexity.

The drawback of a non-stabilised supply is that there can be a vast difference between the loaded and unloaded output voltages. A drop of 30% or so from zero load to full load would by no means be exceptional. This problem can be eased by using a mains transformer of generous current rating, but this obviously increases the bulk and cost of the power supply to some extent.

The practical result of all this is that where an output power rating requires a peak to peak output level of (say) 100 volts, the loaded supply voltage might need to be more like

115 volts, and the unloaded supply could well be as high as 150 volts. To guarantee safe operation, some of the transistors in the amplifier would need to have maximum voltage ratings of around this 150 volt level, not the 100 volts suggested by the peak to peak output potential.

Lower Load Impedance
One approach to high power audio design is to simply use suitably high supply voltages, together with semiconductors having adequate voltage ratings. Power field effect transistors having voltage ratings of around 120 volts to 200 volts are now readily available. These can handle quite high powers of about 100 watts per device, and currents of up to about 7 to 8 amps. These can obviously be used to provide quite high output powers when used in conventional class B output stages. Matching high voltage driver transistors are available for these output transistors.

High voltage bipolar power transistors are also available. Although the ubiquitous 2N3055 is quite popular for audio power amplifier designs, for genuine high power circuits its collector to emitter voltage rating of 60 volts is something of a limitation. Although it is often referred to as a 100 volt transistor, it is only the collector to base rating that is 100 volts. Devices such as the 2N3773/2N6609 complementary pair offer greater scope. These have collector to emitter voltage ratings of 140 volts, collector current ratings of 16 amps, and power ratings of 150 watts.

It can be difficult to obtain really high output powers even with the aid of these "mega" output devices. It is often voltage rather than current ratings that are the limiting factor, and the most simple solution is then to use a lower load impedance. Halving the load impedance from 8 to 4 ohms gives double the current flow, and double the output power (provided the power supply, etc., have suitable ratings). An output power of 300 watts requires about 138 volts peak to peak into 8 ohms, which would probably dictate an unloaded supply voltage in excess of 200 volts (but possibly a little less). For 300 watts r.m.s. into a 4-ohm impedance the required peak to peak voltage is about 97 volts. This would require an unloaded supply voltage of only about 140 volts or so.

6

A slight problem here is that most loudspeakers have an impedance of 8 ohms rather than 4 ohms (although 4-ohm types do exist). However, two 8-ohm loudspeakers wired in parallel give an overall impedance of 4 ohms. Even lower load impedances can be obtained by using more loudspeakers in parallel (four speakers for a load impedance of 2 ohms for example). There is a practical limit to how far you can take this idea. Very low loudspeaker impedances require relatively low drive voltages, but the drive currents can become massive.

Even assuming that everything in the circuit could handle these currents, there are practical difficulties in dealing with such low impedance signals. Very heavy gauge wiring is needed in order to handle currents of ten or twenty amps with low voltage drops. In fact quite heavy gauge wiring is needed to handle such high currents without burning out! Cables to handle very high currents are often more like metal rods than the normal (very flexible) cables we are used to.

Another method of obtaining high output powers from relatively low supply voltages is to use an output transformer (or possibly just an inductor) to provide a suitable voltage step-up. This method has its advantages and drawbacks. One drawback is that it is difficult to produce suitable transformers at reasonable cost. High quality types are expensive — inexpensive types tend to seriously compromise the audio output quality. The main drawback of this method for the home constructor is simply that suitable transformers, or the materials to build your own, do not seem to be readily available. It is only likely to be a practical proposition if you are prepared to improvise with whatever likely looking materials you can obtain, and you are prepared to accept that the final product may not give satisfactory results. Even if suitable materials or components can be obtained, getting this type of circuit to operate well and reliably is not always easy.

Bridge Circuit

A more up-market way of obtaining high powers without having to resort to very high supply voltages is to use a bridge circuit. This does not have to be used as an alternative to a lower load impedance, and it is quite possible to use the two methods together in order to obtain high output powers from quite modest supply voltages. This approach is sometimes used in order to get reasonably high output powers from "transformerless" public address amplifiers which operate on 12-volt batteries.

A bridge amplifier is basically just two power amplifiers driving a single loudspeaker. The arrangement used is outlined in the block diagram of Figure 1.1. Simply driving the two power amplifiers from the same signal, and connecting the loudspeaker from across the two non-earth outputs of the amplifiers, does not provide the desired result. This gives two identical signals across the loudspeaker, as in Figure 1.2. The voltage difference across the outputs of the amplifiers is zero, and no output current flows.

What is needed is anti-phase output signals, as in Figure 1.3. As one signal reaches its peak negative voltage, the other reaches its peak positive potential, and vice versa. For the sake of this example, assume that each output is producing 20 volts peak to peak. Each output is therefore going to maximum positive and negative values of 10 volts. When one output is 10 volts positive, the other is 10 volts negative. This gives a total of 20 volts across the loudspeaker. Half a cycle later the signals have swapped states, and there is again one output at plus 10 volts and one at minus 10 volts. This gives 20 volts across the loudspeaker once more, but this time it has the opposite polarity. With first 20 volts of one polarity, and then

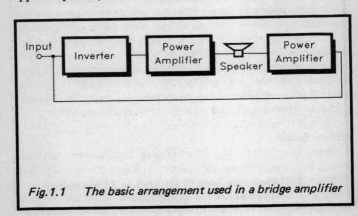

Fig. 1.1   The basic arrangement used in a bridge amplifier

8

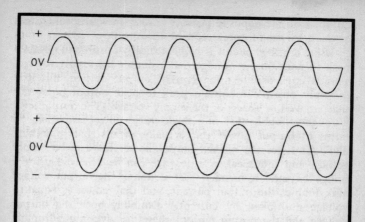

Fig. 1.2 In-phase signals give no voltage difference across the loudspeaker, and zero output

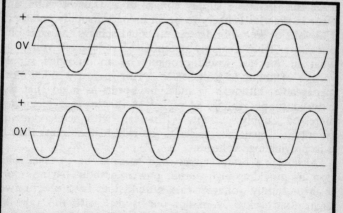

Fig. 1.3 Anti-phase output signals give a large voltage swing across the loudspeaker

20 volts of the opposite polarity across the loudspeaker, this gives a total peak to peak value of 40 volts.

Using a bridge circuit it is theoretically possible to obtain a peak to peak output voltage that is double the supply voltage. This is not possible using current output devices, but it is certainly possible to obtain peak to peak output potentials that are well in excess of the supply voltage. The output level is roughly double that of a single-ended power amplifier. In terms of output power this actually means that something like four times the normal output power for a given supply voltage and loudspeaker impedance can be achieved using a bridge circuit. Remember that doubling the output voltage also doubles the output current, and that power is equal to voltage multiplied by current. Doubling both the output voltage and the output current therefore gives a quadrupling of the output power.

Using a bridge circuit it is clearly possible to obtain quite high output powers without having to resort to either a high supply voltage or extremely low load impedances. As we have already seen, for 100 watts r.m.s. into an 8-ohm impedance loudspeaker some 28.28 volts r.m.s., or 80 volts peak to peak is required. Using a single-ended transformerless output stage this dictates a supply voltage of at least 80 volts, and what in practice is likely to be an unloaded supply voltage of 130 volts or so. A bridge circuit could achieve the same output power from a supply potential of at least 40 volts, and what in practice would probably be an unloaded supply voltage of about 65 volts or so. This is clearly much more manageable, although it must be borne in mind that the reduced supply voltage is gained at the expense of greatly increased supply current. However, with semiconductor circuits it is generally easier to provide high currents than it is to provide high voltages.

Although a bridge circuit may seem to be an ideal solution to providing high output powers without having resort to high supply voltages, this system does have one or two slight drawbacks. A minor one is that with this type of circuit it is generally a little more difficult to obtain good stability than it is with single-ended designs. The probable cause of this is the fact that the input must be in-phase with one of the outputs. This can easily lead to problems with instability due to stray feedback. It is not usually too difficult to obtain good stability though, and this is not a major drawback.

Something that does tend to be a more major problem is that of obtaining a low quiescent output voltage. With this type of circuit it is normal for the output to be directly coupled to the loudspeaker. There is no strong d.c. component across the outputs, which makes using a large electrolytic coupling capacitor a dubious practice. The circuit could be designed to produce a suitably strong polarising voltage, but this would upset the symmetry of the circuit, which would be reflected in a significant reduction in the maximum output power.

Direct coupling is a better way of handling matters, but only if the two output voltages are accurately matched under quiescent conditions. In fact the situation is a little more complex than this, as the output voltages must remain accurately matched when the amplifier is being driven. It is very easy to produce a design that has accurately matched d.c. output potentials under standby conditions, but which has a strong d.c. bias across the outputs when the amplifier is driven hard. It is also easy to produce a design which has accurately matched output levels when it is first set up, but which drifts out of balance within a few minutes.

The problem with d.c. offsets across the output is that they produce strong d.c. flows through the loudspeaker. Apart from reduced efficiency in the amplifier, there are the consequences for the loudspeakers to take into account. Strong d.c. levels maintained for a long period of time can apparently result in the loudspeaker cone being permanently offset from its correct resting position. This could affect the reproduction quality, and would certainly reduce the maximum power level that the unit could handle properly.

Although there are potential problems here, they are not insurmountable. Using operational amplifier style dual balanced supply rails, together with operational amplifier style biasing and feedback circuits, will usually ensure that there is no significant d.c. bias across the outputs.

A small but important point to bear in mind when using

bridge amplifiers is that neither output is at earth potential. Furthermore, as d.c. coupling is used, letting one of the outputs come into electrical contact with the earth rail will produce a massive current flow. The fuses might "blow" in time to prevent any damage, but it is quite likely that one or more output transistors would be destroyed before the fuses cut off the supply. Using dual balanced supplies and a central (0 volt) earth rail can minimise this problem by giving minimal differences between the output potentials and the earth voltage. However, this would not necessarily ensure a low current flow in the event of an output being short circuited to earth.

Power Calculations
Calculating the output power of an audio amplifier should be a simple enough matter, but it is a slightly contentious one. In theory, you simply take the maximum loaded r.m.s. output voltage, square it, and divide by the loudspeaker impedance. For example, 10 volts r.m.s. into an 8-ohm impedance loudspeaker gives 12.5 watts r.m.s. (10 volts squared = 100 volts, divided by 8 ohms = 12.5 watts). If the output voltage is the peak figure, not the r.m.s. one, it should first be divided by 1.414 in order to convert it into an equivalent r.m.s. figure. For peak to peak voltages divide by 2.828 in order to obtain an equivalent r.m.s. value.

While this is all simple enough, in practice matters are complicated by the fact that few audio power amplifiers are powered from stabilised supplies. As already pointed out, the use of stabilised supplies does have potential advantages, but these are normally outweighed by the disadvantages. In particular, the increased cost and bulk. An advantage of a non-stabilised supply is that it enables short spiky waveforms to be handled better. Although waveforms of this type give very high peak output powers, they produce relatively low current consumptions. Figure 1.4 helps to illustrate this point.

In the upper waveform, which is triangular, the average level is just half the peak level. In the lower waveform its spiky nature means that the average level is only about one-tenth of the peak level. The peak output power is the same

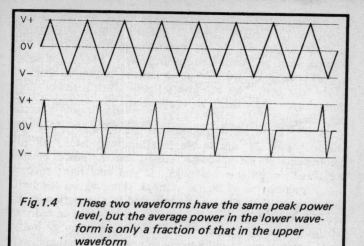

Fig. 1.4   These two waveforms have the same peak power
level, but the average power in the lower waveform is only a fraction of that in the upper
waveform

for both waveforms, but the average output power (and
current consumption) are much lower for the pulsed waveform. This means that the supply voltage sags relatively
little on a pulsed signal, permitting higher peak output powers
to be produced. Provided the output transistors have suitably
high ratings, on this type of signal relatively high peak output
powers can be handled before the onset of clipping.

In a similar vein, it is possible for an amplifier having a
non-stabilised supply to provide higher than normal output
powers, even with sinewave signals, if they are only supplied
in intermittent bursts. This is simply due to the fact that
the smoothing capacitors in the power supply circuit will
have very high values, and at a middle audio frequency or
higher it takes several cycles before these capacitors become
significantly discharged and the supply voltage sags. An
amplifier might provide 100 watts r.m.s. with a continuous
signal, but perhaps about 150 watts r.m.s. or more if it is fed
with short bursts of sinewave signal.

This has led to some imaginative output power ratings over
the years, particularly for hi-fi amplifiers. Output powers
quoted as "continuous r.m.s." in some cases turned out to be

figures for something like five cycles at 1 kHz. In other words, "continuous" actually meant for about 5 milliseconds! Some quoted output powers are even less justifiable than this. Ratings such as "combined music power" seem to be some sort of peak figure, with the powers of the two stereo channels added together. This can give a figure which is ten or more times higher than the true continuous r.m.s. output power per channel.

In this book all output powers are in watts r.m.s. per channel, and are sustainable indefinitely provided all the components are of adequate ratings, and the power devices are fitted on suitable heatsinks. If you take short cuts by using components of inferior ratings, skimping on the heatsinking, etc., then this will be reflected in a reduction in the available output power. It will also be reflected in reduced reliability. Using components of inadequate rating, or inadequate heatsinking, is quite likely to result in something overheating and being destroyed if the amplifier is run at high power for a period of time. The power ratings in this book only apply if a power supply circuit of adequate rating is used. Remember that the power rating of an amplifier is as much dependent on the power supply as it is on the amplifier itself.

When comparing the power ratings of these circuits with those of other high power amplifiers, remember to check exactly what form the output powers of the amplifiers are given in. Unless you know this, output power ratings do not really tell you a great deal.

14

Chapter 2

BIPOLAR OR MOSFET

Up until about ten years ago, the choice when designing a high power audio amplifier was between bipolar transistors or valves. Even in those days, the valve option was not a popular one. Whatever the relative merits of valves and transistors in high power audio applications (and valves do have their advantages where high powers are involved), valves were not a popular choice due to difficulties in obtaining the necessary components. These days the component buying problems are that much greater, rendering home constructed valve amplifier projects something that are only suitable for the dedicated few.

These days there is a real alternative to bipolar transistors in the form of power field effect transistors (f.e.t.s). The two commonly available forms of power f.e.t. are the VMOS and the power MOSFET types. High power VMOS transistors suitable for operation in high power audio amplifiers are produced, but these are not very readily available. Also, complementary devices suitable for genuinely symmetrical class B output stages are very difficult to obtain. Quasi-symmetrical output stages using only n channel devices (the f.e.t equivalent to n.p.n. bipolar transistors) are possible, but the lack of true symmetry can compromise performance.

For audio applications the Hitachi power MOSFETs are probably the better choice. These are somewhat more expensive than VMOS devices, and are substantially more expensive than most bipolar power transistors. On the other hand, they have high voltage, current, and power ratings, and bipolar devices that are true alternatives to these power f.e.t.s are not exactly cheap. Even if power f.e.t.s are somewhat more expensive, as we shall see, they probably more than justify their extra cost. They can be used in relatively simple circuits, provide a very high reproduction quality, and offer excellent reliability. They are particularly well suited to home constructed amplifiers as they avoid any complicated setting-up procedures.

15

Class B

In order to understand the merits of power MOSFETs it is first necessary to understand the basic way in which class B output stages operate. In early transistor designs there were usually two transformers (a driver and an output type). Later configurations avoided the need for one or other of these, and eventually "transformerless" complementary output stages were developed. A basic class B audio amplifier of this type uses the configuration of Figure 2.1. This circuit has a direct coupled output with dual balanced supplies and a central 0 volt earth rail. In practice there is often a single supply rail and a capacitive coupling to the loudspeaker. The basic way in which the circuit operates is much the same in either case, but the direct coupled version is probably the easier to understand.

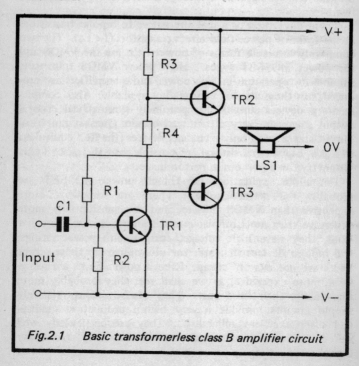

Fig.2.1   Basic transformerless class B amplifier circuit

16

TR1 is the driver transistor, and it operates as a straight-forward common emitter amplifier having the series resistance of R3 and R4 as its collector load resistance. The reason for having this split load resistance will be explained later. TR2 and TR3 are the complementary output transistors, and these operate in the emitter follower mode. Unlike the driver stage, they provide no voltage gain, but they do provide a large amount of current gain. They therefore act as buffers which enable the high drive currents required by the loudspeaker to be satisfied.

Biasing of the whole circuit is provided by R1 and R2, which must set the quiescent output voltage accurately at the central 0 volt supply level. With a d.c. coupled circuit this requires the use of a preset resistor to enable the d.c. output potential to be trimmed to precisely the correct level. This is not always necessary with capacitvely coupled circuits, where the output coupling capacitor prevents any strong direct current flow if the biasing is not spot-on.

Negative feedback is applied over the circuit via the bias resistors. This reduces the circuit's voltage gain, and also helps to reduce noise and distortion. C1 provides d.c. blocking at the input of the circuit.

On positive output excursions TR3 is cut off, but TR2 is biased into conduction and supplies current to the loud-speaker. On negative output excursions it is TR2 that is cut off, and TR3 that supplies the drive current to the loud-speaker. The higher the output voltage on half cycles of either polarity, the higher the current that is drawn from the appropriate supply rail.

This type of circuit might seem to be unnecessarily compli-cated, offering no obvious advantage over a simple class A type. However, with a class A output stage there is a constant and very high current consumption. Even if the amplifier would always be run continuously at full power, a class A output stage would not offer a very high level of efficiency. In fact most of the supply current tends to end up in the output transistor and the load circuit, rather than in the loudspeaker. Class A output stages often offer efficiencies of only about 20% to 25%. Of course, in practice no audio power amplifier is driven continuously at full power by a

17

sinewave input signal, and the true efficiency is likely to be only a few percent.

When driven continuously at full power, class B output stages can provide theoretical efficiencies of around the 70% mark. Practical circuits will often fall well short of the theoretical maximum efficiency level, but will still be far superior to class A designs in this respect. This means that for a given output power they require smaller power supplies, and less heatsinking on the output transistors. They consequently tend to be smaller and cheaper than class A designs, despite what are usually more complex output stages. Unlike class A designs, class B output stages do not consume a high power level when there is little or no output signal. The current consumption is proportional to the output power, and is zero with no input signal. As we shall see shortly, practical designs normally have some quiescent current flow through the output transistors, but this is usually only a small fraction of the quiescent current drain of a class A circuit of similar output power.

Cross-over Distortion

Class B amplifiers might seem to be too good to be true, and as one might expect, there is a catch. This is in the form of cross-over distortion. This is a severe type of distortion which is at its worst at low power levels, where distortion tends to be most noticeable. The problem arises because transistors do not start to conduct as soon as a forward bias voltage is applied. For silicon bipolar transistors it is normally necessary for the bias voltage to reach something like 0.5 to 0.6 volts before the device starts to conduct. Thereafter, only a small increase in the bias voltage is needed in order to cause the device to conduct heavily.

If we apply this to our simple class B amplifier circuit of Figure 2.1, it means that the collector of TR1 has to swing about 0.5 to 0.6 volts positive or negative before the output voltage will start to change at all. If we apply this to a triangular output waveform, the correct output waveform is shown in Figure 2.2 (top). The lower waveform is how the output signal might actually appear. This distortion looks bads, and sounds even worse!

18

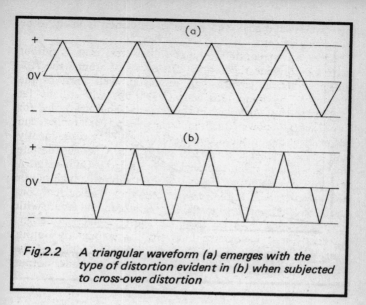

Fig.2.2   *A triangular waveform (a) emerges with the type of distortion evident in (b) when subjected to cross-over distortion*

A forward bias is normally applied to the output transistors under quiescent conditions in order to counteract cross-over distortion. This is the purpose of R4. In practice it is not good enough to merely bring the output transistors to the brink of conduction. A bipolar transistor has a relatively low gain as it initially switches on. The gain steadily increases as the collector current is increased, and then flattens out at fairly high currents. It might then actually drop away slightly at very high currents. A typical transfer characteristic might look something like the graph of Figure 2.3 (which is actually exaggerated slightly in order to emphasise the non-linearity of a transistor).

This means that in practice an amplifier based on bipolar transistors, or any other amplifying device available at present come to that, can never offer complete freedom from distortion. The amplifier must be designed to keep the innate distortion level as low as possible, with negative feedback then being used to reduce the actual distortion level of the circuit to an acceptable figure. Negative feedback can reduce

19

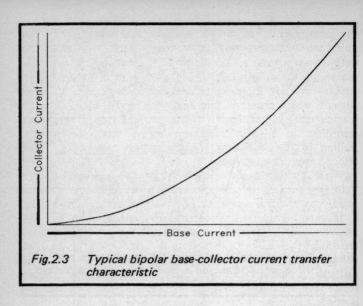

Fig.2.3   Typical bipolar base-collector current transfer characteristic

distortion levels by substantial amounts, but it is not a total solution. With an innate distortion level, that is (say) 2% or less, negative feedback which produces a 40dB reduction in gain (i.e. reduces the voltage gain by a factor of one hundred) will also reduce the distortion levels by a factor of one hundred. This would give an impressive distortion figure of 0.02% or less. Using a small quiescent bias through the output transistors is not likely to give an innate distortion figure of 2% though. At low signal levels it would probably be around 50% or more! Even with a substantial 40dB of feedback, this would still leave some 0.5% or more distortion.

Thermal Runaway
Using a higher bias current will still leave a reasonably low quiescent current consumption, and will not significantly affect the efficiency of the amplifier. However, it will lead to problems with thermal runaway. The important fact to bear in mind here is that the threshold voltage of a bipolar transistor is temperature dependent. The higher the temperature of

the component, the lower its threshold voltage. If the quiescent bias current is set at the correct level while the output transistors are cool, as they heat up in use, the quiescent current will climb. This can result in a regenerative action where the increased heat causes an increase in the bias current, which causes further heating, a further increase in the bias current, and so on. The bias current steadily increases regardless of whether the amplifier is driven, eventually leading to the destruction of the output transistors. This effect is thermal runaway.

With any class B amplifier of this general type and of more than very modest output power, it is essential to take steps to counteract thermal runaway. This is sometimes achieved using a negative temperature coefficient thermistor in the R4 position. This detects any increase in temperature, and its resistance then falls. This results in a reduction in the bias voltage, which stabilises the bias current. In practice it is difficult to find a thermistor that maintains the bias current reasonably accurately. Only very slight under-compensation is needed in order to let thermal runaway still occur, albeit more slowly than would otherwise be the case. Slight over-compensation will reduce the bias current, giving noticeable cross-over distortion.

The more modern approach is to use two diodes, as in Figure 2.4, or a transistor in the so-called "amplified diode" configuration, as shown in Figure 2.5. The two diodes are forward biased, and act rather like low voltage zener diodes. About 0.6 volts is needed in order to bring each one into conduction, but only a marginally higher voltage is needed in order to produce a strong current flow. This gives a voltage of about 1.3 volts across the two diodes, which is about right to give a moderate quiescent current flow through the output transistors.

In practice the diodes are mounted very close to the output transistors, and might even be mounted on their heatsink. The diodes therefore quickly respond to any change in the temperature of the output transistors. Like the threshold voltages of the output transistors, the threshold potentials of the diodes are temperature dependent. Increases in temperature cause a reduction in their "zener" voltage, and tend to counteract any

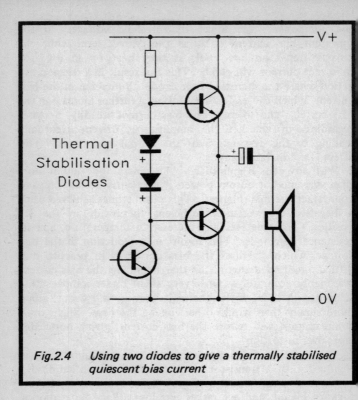

Fig.2.4   *Using two diodes to give a thermally stabilised quiescent bias current*

increase in the output bias current. Provided the diodes are suitable silicon types, they will have thermal characteristics that are a good match for the output transistors, and which give a stable quiescent current.

The problem with this simple method of stabilisation is that there is no certainty that the bias current will be stabilised at a suitable level. Ideally it should be possible to trim the quiescent output current to a suitable figure, which is possible using the amplified diode method of stabilisation. This simple configuration gives what is a sort of variable zener diode. If the preset resistor provides half the collector voltage to the base terminal, then it will stabilise the emitter to collector voltage at about double the base voltage. This gives a "zener"

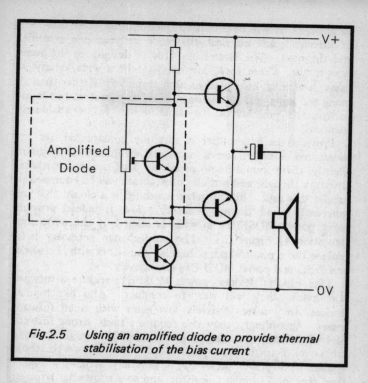

Fig.2.5   *Using an amplified diode to provide thermal
stabilisation of the bias current*

voltage of about 1.3 volts, like the two diode circuit. However, by adjusting the preset resistor it is possible to trim the
voltage substantially either side of this figure, permitting
practically any desired quiescent output current to be set.
The "zener" voltage is a factor of the base voltage, and
increases in temperature cause the collector and base voltages
to drop. This gives the required thermal stabilisation of the
quiescent bias current, and provided the transistor in the
amplified diode circuit is a suitable silicon type, very accurate
stabilisation will be obtained.

Power MOSFETs
This is all very well in theory, but in practice it can be difficult
to obtain really stable bias levels. It is easier when designing

amplifiers that will be produced commercially, since there will be no significant physical difference between one amplifier and the next. The same is not true of designs for the home constructor, where there are likely to be a wide variety of cases, heatsinks, etc., used in each amplifier. Rather than all being the same, it would be reasonable to expect no two home constructed projects of the same design to be absolutely identical!

Provided each amplifier is carefully constructed, set up, monitored initially, and if necessary readjusted or modified slightly, there should be no problem. This is a less than ideal situation though, and not all constructors will be equipped to handle this task. Ideally what is needed is a circuit that has inherently good thermal stability. This is indeed possible using power MOSFETs in what is essentially the same configuration as Figure 2.1. The only change necessary is to replace the n.p.n. and p.n.p. bipolar transistors with N channel and P channel power MOSFETs respectively.

Like bipolar devices, power MOSFETs require a forward bias before they will start to conduct. Also like bipolar devices, they offer relatively low gains with small forward biases. Accordingly, they also require a fairly strong forward bias when used in a class B power amplifier circuit if strong cross-over distortion is to be avoided. The forward threshold voltage of a power MOSFET is generally somewhat higher than that of a bipolar transistor, and so a somewhat stronger bias voltage is normally needed.

One of the big advantages of power MOSFETs is that they have a positive temperature coefficient at low currents, but a negative type at medium and high currents. If the quiescent current is set at a low level, as the output transistors heat up, the bias current increases slightly. However, it does not increase very much, since the quiescent current soon reaches the turn-over point where the temperature coefficient becomes negative. Further increases in temperature then cause a slight reduction in the quiescent bias current. This changeover from a positive to a negative temperature coefficient tends to stabilise the quiescent current quite close to the current at which the changeover occurs.

In practice the power f.e.t.s that are intended for class B

audio power use are designed to have a changeover current which is a good choice for the quiescent bias level (typically about 60 to 100 milliamps). This results in excellent thermal stability without the need for any temperature compensation circuits. In fact the inherent thermal stability of a power MOSFET output stage means that any attempt to provide a thermal stabilisation circuit would probably make matters worse rather than better. For the home constructor the absence of any problems with thermal stability, and getting compensation circuits set up correctly, obviously makes life very much easier. If nothing else, it gives peace of mind as there is no risk whatever of thermal runaway occurring with this type of output stage.

Parallel Operation

There is a potential problem with using bipolar transistors at high powers, and this is secondary breakdown. Basically this means that there are voltage and current combinations which are not acceptable, even though they are within the device's V_{ceo} and I_c ratings, and will not result in excessive power and heat dissipation. Apparently this is due to a sort of localised thermal runaway causing "hot-spots" in the semiconductor structure. The effect of these "hot-spots" is to cause a virtual short circuit from the collector to the emitter, resulting in the rapid destruction of the device. Due to their negative temperature coefficient at high operating currents, power MOSFETs do not suffer from secondary breakdown. Whereas bipolar power transistors often have to be used well within their maximum voltage and current ratings in order to operate reliably, power MOSFETs can be used right up to both ratings without any risk of them being damaged (provided the power ratings are not exceeded of course).

A practical benefit of this absence of secondary breakdown is that it is possible to use power MOSFETs safely in parallel. In other words, each output transistor can actually consist of two devices connected in the manner shown in Figure 2.6. This shares the current between the two transistors in each parallel pair, permitting higher output currents and powers to be handled. In fact by using this arrangement it is possible to halve the loudspeaker impedance, and double the output power.

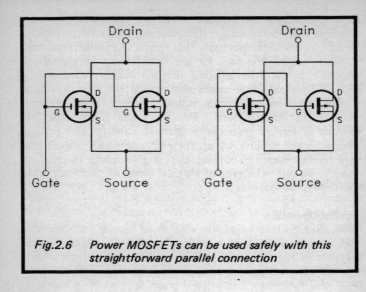

Fig.2.6   Power MOSFETs can be used safely with this straightforward parallel connection

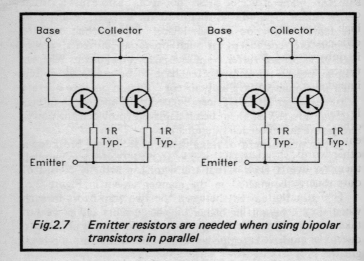

Fig.2.7   Emitter resistors are needed when using bipolar transistors in parallel

This is actually a slight over-simplification, and for this method to be fully successful it is necessary to have a driver circuit that can take the additional loading of the extra output transistors. This is not difficult with power MOSFETs, since they have the high input impedances associated with all f.e.t. devices. The input capacitance of power MOSFETs precludes the use of true micro-power driver stages, which would give an inadequate high frequency response due to the capacitive loading of the output stage. A driver current of only about 10 milliamps is normally adequate though.

The very low drive currents required by power MOSFETs gives them a major advantage over bipolar transistors. In order to obtain comparable gain at least two bipolar transistors have to be used. The Darlington pair configuration is probably the more popular configuration, but the twin common emitter type with 100% negative feedback is also used to a significant degree. Both configurations effectively provide a single transistor having a current gain equal to the products of the two gains of the individual transistors in the pair. For instance, if the current gains of the two transistors in a pair are 50 and 60, they effectively provide a single transistor having a current gain of 3000 (50 × 60 = 3000). Even so, quite high drive currents of a few hundred milliamps are often needed in very high power circuits. Bear in mind here that in order to work efficiently, the amplifier must have an output impedance that is only a small fraction of the loudspeaker impedance. A typical medium or high power audio amplifier has an output impedance of a few milliohms or less.

With power MOSFETs the parallel arrangement is inherently stable. If one device tends to draw more current than the other, it heats up more, but the negative temperature coefficient results in it taking a lower proportion of the current. In other words, the characteristics of power MOSFETs results in them tending to stabilise with an almost identical share of the output current.

The situation is very different with bipolar transistors when they are used in a similar arrangement. If one device takes more current than the other, it heats up more, which due to its positive temperature coefficient results in it taking a greater proportion of the output current. This results in it heating up still further, taking an even greater share of the output current. The other device takes an ever decreasing proportion of the output current, which results in it operating cooler. This in turn causes it to take a lower proportion of the output current. Rather than tending to stabilise with an even share of the output current, the tendency is for one device to take an ever increasing share of the output current, while the other takes less and less. This is quite likely to ultimately result in the destruction of the output transistor that takes the "lion's share" of the output current.

The normal way around this problem is to use emitter resistors, as in Figure 2.7. Output currents flow through these resistors, causing voltages to be produced across them. These voltages effectively raise the base to emitter voltage needed for a given collector current. The higher this current the higher the required base to emitter voltage becomes. If one transistor takes a higher share of the current flow, this results in its effective base to emitter threshold voltage increasing. At the same time, the other device takes a lower current, and its effective base to emitter turn on potential reduces. This tends to reduce the current through the device that takes the higher current, and increase the flow through the transistor that takes the lower current. In other words, it tends to even out any discrepancies in the two current flows. Provided the resistors are high enough in value, and the gains of the transistors are not too dissimilar, this will ensure stable operation of the circuit. Incidentally, these emitter resistors are sometimes included when single output transistors are used. It helps to guard against thermal runaway.

In practice it is undesirable to include these resistors because they produce voltage drops. These voltage drops are reflected in a reduction in the output voltage swing. In practice this is the price that has to be paid in order to obtain reliable operation. In fairness, it has to be admitted that the "on" resistances of power MOSFETs tend to be higher than the equivalent figures for bipolar transistors. Thus, even with these resistors added, pairs of bipolar transistors might actually provide lower "on" resistances than pairs of power MOSFETs. Note that if bipolar transistors are used in parallel pairs, it is normal for each pair to be mounted on the same heatsink. This gives a thermal coupling between the two devices, which helps to discourage any creeping apart of their relative shares of the output current.

Although we have only been talking here in terms of pairs of transistors connected in parallel, it is possible to use any desired number of transistors in parallel. In practice though, there may be no point in doing so. The more transistors that are connected in parallel, the greater the drive current that is needed. This could lead to an impractical collector current being needed in the driver stage. Probably the main point to bear in mind is that this method only permits higher output currents to be obtained — not higher output voltages. It is possible that the parallel transistors would produce lower voltage drops, and would give slightly boosted output voltage swings. This would be more likely to occur with power MOSFETs than bipolar transistors, since the voltage drops across single power MOSFETs are often quite high. This is due to their relatively high "on" resistances. However, this effect is not likely to produce a boost in output power of more than a few percent.

The doubling in the output current, provided the power supply has a suitably high current rating to give this increased current, gives a doubling of output power. This is only obtained by halving the load impedance though. In practice there will be a limit on minimum load impedance that can be used. This often precludes the use of more than two devices in parallel, but it is worthwhile remembering that more devices can be used if necessary.

Speed

In the early days of power transistors there was a major problem in getting the devices to operate at speeds that would enable them to be used in practical applications. For high frequency operation it is necessary to make transistors physically small, but in order to permit high powers to be handled they must be physically large (or relatively so anyway). This makes it difficult to obtain both high power and high operating speed. Most of the early power transistors were barely usable in low quality audio applications, and only a few "specials" were capable of operating at radio frequencies. Most of these radio frequency devices would only operate up to a few megahertz.

Matters improved when silicon transistors took over and the original germanium devices became obsolete. Even so, many high power bipolar transistors have low F_t ratings, and are prone to problems with slewing induced distortion (or SID as it is often termed). This is where a strong high frequency signal requires the output voltage to change at a high rate which is beyond the capabilities of the output transistors. These signal conditions may only occur infrequently, but the resultant distortion can be quite severe, and very noticeable indeed.

The high frequency performance of good quality power devices designed specifically for operation in audio power amplifiers is usually much better than that of general purpose high power devices such as the ever popular 2N3055. The cost is generally somewhat more, but the difference is not usually large enough to greatly affect the overall cost of the finished amplifier complete with power supply. Most of the cost is usually accounted for by the mains transformer, massive heatsinks, the case, etc., rather than the semiconductors. Where really high output powers are required, there may be no option but to resort to very high power devices having quite low F_t figures (usually only about 200kHz). Although a figure of about 200kHz might seem perfectly adequate for the 20 kHz audio bandwidth, remember that this is not the frequency at which the gain starts to fall away. It is the frequency at which the gain falls to unity, which really means it is the frequency at which the device ceases to offer any worthwhile gain at all!

Of course, in many high power audio applications the audio quality might be of secondary importance to the output power, and something short of true hi-fi performance may be quite acceptable. In particular, if the amplifier will only be required to handle voice signals, slewing induced distortion is not likely to be a significant consideration. Any slewing induced distortion that should occur will not matter very much, and the nature of the input signal is such that there is little likelihood of this type of distortion occurring anyway.

A factor that could still cause problems is the significant phase lag that occurs through a relatively slow output stage. This results in feedback that should be of the negative variety being inverted and converted into positive feedback. In a minor case this could result in "ringing" and other relatively mild forms of high frequency instability. In a severe case it results in the circuit breaking into oscillation — usually at an ultrasonic frequency. This problem is avoided in practice by using so-called "compensation" components, which can be anything from a single low value capacitor through to several C — R circuits. With a very slow output stage the high frequency response of the circuit might have to be rolled-off at quite a low frequency, possibly severely attenuating the higher audio frequencies. Again, this will not matter if the amplifier is only required to handle voice signals, but it would clearly be a major drawback where music signals are involved.

Slewing induced distortion is less of a problem if power MOSFETs are used in the output stage. These have relatively high operating speeds, and are typically some fifty to one hundred times faster than silicon power transistors having similar power ratings. This is normally sufficient to totally eliminate any problems with slewing induced distortion, or inadequate bandwidth due to the use of heavy frequency compensation. In fact power MOSFET based amplifiers will often operate with good stability even if no frequency compensation circuit is used. In practice it is normal for such a circuit to be included. This is done in order to avoid problems such as the breakthrough of radio frequency signals picked up in the input wiring.

Most audio power amplifiers use configurations that are more complicated than the one of Figure 2.1. This configuration is simple, but it has a number of flaws. One of these is that it does not have a very high innate (open loop) voltage gain, leaving little scope for reducing distortion by using large amounts of negative feedback. It does not have a particularly low innate distortion level either. Practical circuits normally have two common emitter stages ahead of the output stage in order to boost the open loop voltage gain to a more useful level. In order to reduce the distortion of the driver stage it is often equipped with a constant current source as its collector load, in place of a simple resistor. For the same reason, the input stage is often a "long tailed pair" rather than a simple common emitter stage. We will deal with some of these improved configurations in the next chapter, which covers some practical amplifier circuits plus suitable mains power supply units.

Chapter 3

HIGH POWER CIRCUITS

So far we have only talked in fairly broad and rather theoretical terms. In this chapter some practical high power audio amplifier circuits will be described, complete with suitable printed circuit board designs in some cases. Although these circuits can probably be constructed by anyone who has a certain amount of experience at electronic project construction, I must emphasise that I do not consider these designs to be suitable for those of limited experience at this type of thing. High power audio amplifiers tend to be very unforgiving if mistakes are made, and even those who have many years of experience at project construction need to proceed carefully with these (or any other) high power audio circuits.

Configuration

The basic class A driver and class B output stage described in Chapter 2 will work in practice, but will not give particularly good results. The open loop voltage gain of this simple arrangement is quite low, giving little scope for the application of negative feedback in order to improve performance. An extra stage of amplification is needed in order to overcome this problem, and give better results. Figure 3.1 shows what is generally considered to be the most simple configuration that is capable of providing reasonably good results. This is shown as having a pair of power MOSFETs in the class B output stage, but this configuration can obviously be used with a complementary bipolar output stage if preferred.

The driver and output stages are much the same as in the basic configuration described in Chapter 2. The difference is in the addition of a common emitter stage (TR1) at the input of the circuit. This has its output direct coupled to the input of the driver stage, making the entire circuit direct coupled (apart from the d.c. blocking capacitors at the input and output, of course). Although a common emitter amplifier would normally be expected to provide a very high level of voltage gain (typically about 50dB for a high gain silicon

33

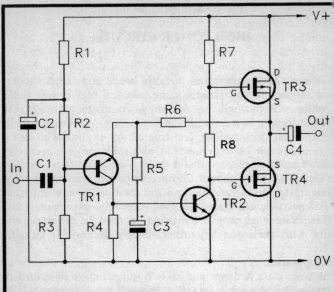

Fig.3.1 *The most simple power amplifier configuration that will provide reasonably good results*

device), the overall voltage gain of this circuit is just unity This is due to the 100% negative feedback from the output t the emitter of TR1, via R6. R1, R2 and R3 are used to bia the input of the circuit to about half the supply voltage, whic in turn gives the required output bias level of half the suppl potential. R1 and C2 act as a so-called "hum" filter, whic prevent any mains "hum" or other noise on the supply line from being coupled to the input of the amplifier via the bia ing network.

In order to give the circuit a useful voltage gain at audi frequencies it is necessary to remove some of the negativ feedback at these frequencies. The feedback must not b altered at d.c., since this would upset the biasing condition. C3 decouples the feedback at audio frequencies, but provide d.c. blocking that leaves the biasing unaltered. R5 limits th amount of feedback that is removed, and therefore controls the closed loop voltage gain of the circuit. This operates in a similar manner to an operational amplifier used in the non-inverting mode, and the voltage gain is equal to (R5 + R6) divided by R5. The open loop gain of the circuit is likely to be quite high at (typically) about 70dB. This means that the circuit can have a useful closed loop gain of around 30dB while still having about 40dB of feedback to reduce the distortion to an acceptable level.

Practical Circuit

The circuit diagram of Figure 3.2 is for a practical power amplifier based on the configuration of Figure 3.1. This follows the original configuration quite closely, but it has a few refinements. At the input of the circuit, R1 and C4 provide a simple lowpass filter action. This removes any high frequency signals that might be present on the input signal, and which could otherwise cause unwanted audio break-through or other problems. C5 provides a small amount of high frequency roll-off which helps to avoid problems with high frequency instability. R10 and C9 are included for the same reason, and they are needed to compensate for the highly inductive nature of a loudspeaker, which represents an awkward load.

In the driver stage the simple load resistor for TR3 has been replaced with a constant current generator based on TR2. A constant current load has certain advantages, such as improved linearity from the driver stage. The constant current source sets the operating current of the driver stage at only about 8 milliamps, but this is adequate for the power MOSFET output stage. VR1 enables the quiescent output current to be adjusted, and in practice it should be adjusted for a bias level of about 80 milliamps. The specified values for R7 and R5 give a closed loop voltage gain of a little under 26dB. This means that about 4 volts peak to peak is needed at the input in order to fully drive the amplifier. If necessary, the gain can be boosted somewhat by making R7 higher in value (increases in its value giving a proportionate boost in gain). This will result in a slight increase in the noise and distortion figures though.

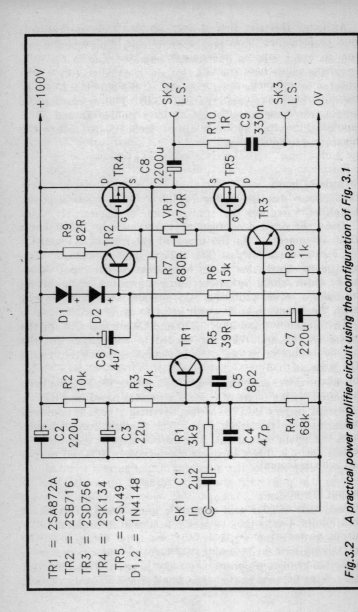

Fig.3.2 A practical power amplifier circuit using the configuration of Fig. 3.1

TR1 = 2SA872A
TR2 = 2SB716
TR3 = 2SD756
TR4 = 2SK134
TR5 = 2SJ49
D1,2 = 1N4148

36

Although this amplifier is very simple, it provides quite good performance. I would not claim true hi-fi performance from it, but I suppose it is true to say that it betters many amplifiers which have claimed this status. Provided it is not driven into clipping, the distortion level should be only a fraction of 1% at any power level. This includes very low powers where many otherwise excellent amplifiers give disappointing results. It has an open loop voltage gain (and therefore a feedback level) which is virtually constant over the audio range, resulting in a distortion performance which is much the same over the full audio spectrum. The same is not true of many power amplifiers which have bipolar output transistors, where there is often a marked loss of performance at high audio frequencies.

The unweighted signal to noise ratio should be better than 80dB, assuming that the "hum" content is minimal. The value of C3 can be increased to give better "hum" filtering at the input, if this should prove to be necessary. Pick-up of "hum" on the input wiring is a more likely cause of problems, and this can be avoided by using a good quality screened lead to make the connections between the circuit board and SK1.

The maximum output power depends on the load impedance and the supply voltage used. I would recommend that the unloaded supply voltage should not exceed about 100 volts. In the components list the maximum operating voltages of the electrolytic capacitors are given on the basis that the supply voltage will never exceed this figure. Apart from this factor, the maximum collector — emitter voltage ratings of the transistors must be taken into account. All three bipolar devices have a rating of 120 volts (the output devices have a maximum drain-to-source voltage rating of 140 volts incidentally).

Output Power

With the specified supply potential of 100 volts, and an 8 ohm loudspeaker, the circuit should comfortably achieve an output power of more than 50 watts r.m.s. Note that we are talking here in terms of a genuinely continuous r.m.s. rating, and not some form of transient power rating. We are also talking here in terms of the output power below the point at which there is any hint of clipping. Where very low distortion is not needed, the circuit can be pushed to somewhat higher power levels. Adjusting the value of R3 to give symmetrical clipping (with a loaded output) can also help to optimise the power performance, although it might not make much difference to the perceived volume level provided by the amplifier. With the biasing optimised, and the amplifier driven to the point where the distortion level is a few percent the output power should be somewhere in the region of 75 watts r.m.s. Again, we are talking here in terms of a true continuous r.m.s. level.

This amplifier's output power is somewhat less than one might expect, given that the supply potential is about 100 volts and the load impedance is 8 ohms. It would seem to be reasonable to expect an output voltage swing of about 80 volts or more, which equates with an r.m.s. output power of over 100 watts. However, as explained previously, the "on" resistance of a power MOSFET is rather high by the standards of high power semiconductors, and this results in voltage drop that significantly reduce the maximum output voltage swing It should also be borne in mind that 100 volts is the unloaded supply voltage, and that it will "sag" slightly when fully loaded.

In order to obtain higher output powers the power supply can have a mains transformer with a higher current rating than the minimum requirement, so as to minimise the loading of the supply voltage at high output powers. Another method is to use pairs of parallel connected power MOSFETs in the output stage. This reduces the voltage drops through the output stage, and boosts the output voltage swing quite significantly. If both these methods are adopted, the circuit should be able to manage at least 80 watts r.m.s. without too much difficulty, and will probably be able to exceed 100 watts r.m.s. before the onset of severe clipping and serious distortion.

Taking things one step further, the load impedance can be reduced to 4 ohms. In conjunction with parallel pairs in the output stage, and a suitably hefty mains transformer in the power supply, this should permit output powers of over 150 watts r.m.s. to be achieved. I have not extensively tested the

mplifier under these conditions, but some quick checks
would suggest that an output power of around 160 watts at
reasonably low distortion is quite achievable. Although you
might think that halving the load impedance would double
the maximum output power from around 100 watts r.m.s. to
about 200 watts r.m.s., matters are not quite as simple as this.
Reducing the load impedance increases the voltage drops
through the output stage, and prevents this simple doubling
up of the output power. Using further output transistors in
parallel with the existing ones will rectify this problem.

Note though, that using several parallel connected devices
for each output transistor gives an increase in the input capaci-
ance of the output stage, which effectively rolls-off the high
frequency gain of the driver stage. This is reflected in a
degradation of the distortion performance at high frequencies.
However, this problem is not likely to result in a serious loss
of performance, and is a perfectly practical approach if it is
important to squeeze as much power out of the unit as
possible. By doing this it should be possible to obtain about
200 watts r.m.s. into a 4-ohm impedance load, but I must
stress that I have not tried this in practice, and can not
guarantee that it will give the desired result.

Power Supply

A suitable mains power supply circuit for the MOSFET
power amplifier is shown in Figure 3.3. This is an entirely
conventional circuit using a fullwave bridge rectifier. It is
assumed that the mains plug will be fitted with a 2-amp or
3-amp fuse. If not, then a 2-amp fuse should be included in
the power supply circuit in series with S1a. Do not omit the
3-amp fuse at the output of the supply, as this is the only
overload protection for the circuit. You might care to add a
3-amp fuse in one of the secondary leads of T1. This would
give protection against a fault in C1 or the bridge rectifier.
Note though, that this fuse would have to be of the anti-surge
type, and not of the more usual "quick-blow" variety. A
"quick-blow" fuse would almost certainly live up to its name
at switch-on, due to the high surge current as C1 took up its
initial charge.

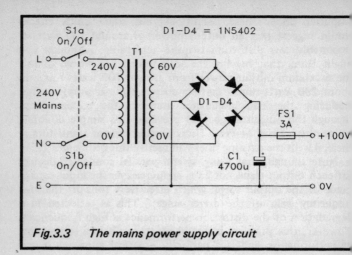

Fig.3.3   The mains power supply circuit

The minimum suitable current rating for T1 depends on the way in which the power amplifier is used. Two amps should be adequate if the unit is used with an 8-ohm impedance loudspeaker, even if it is likely to be driven fairly heavily. A rating of 3 amps is preferable if the unit will be used with parallel pairs in the output stage and driven heavily. If parallel pairs in the output stage plus a 4-ohm load impedance are used, then a rating of 4 amps or more would be necessary. With multiple output transistors and a 4-ohm load, a current rating of around 5 amps would be preferable. It would also be necessary to use a 5-amp fuse for FS1, and C1 would preferably be increased to 10000μ in value (or two 4700μ capacitors connected in parallel could be used). D1 to D4 have a rating of 3 amps, and would need to be replaced with components having ratings of at least 200 volts and 5 amps. Although the bridge rectifier is shown as being made up from four individual rectifiers, it is perfectly acceptable to use a ready-made bridge rectifier assembly having suitable voltage and current ratings.

For stereo operation I would recommend having separate power supplies for the two amplifiers. S1 would, of course, be common to both supplies, and the mains transformer could be

40

a type having twin secondaries, one for each supply circuit. The other components would have to be duplicated in the two supply circuits.

Construction

A suitable printed circuit design for the MOSFET power amplifier is shown in Figure 3.4 (copper track pattern) and Figure 3.5 (component overlay). Construction of the board follows the usual lines and should not present any difficulties. There are several points which must be kept in mind when dealing with the overall construction of the amplifier though. R10 and C9 are not fitted on the board, but are connected across the loudspeaker sockets (SK2 and SK3), where they should be most effective. SK2 and SK3 should be a type of

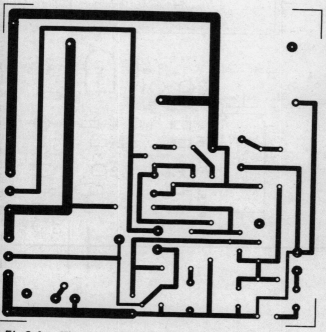

Fig.3.4   *The copper track pattern for the MOSFET power amplifier*

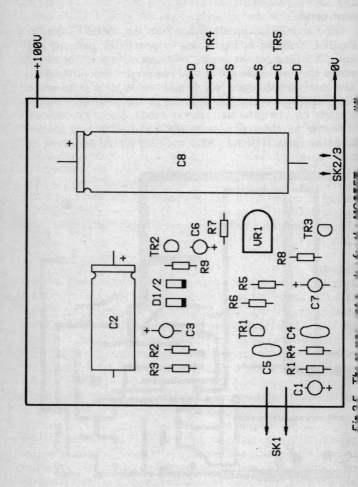

Fig 3.5 The component side of the MOSFET ...

42

socket suitable for heavy duty applications. Terminal posts and heavy duty spring terminals are good choices for applications of this type. The supply wiring and the leads to SK2 and SK3 should be completed using a heavy duty connecting wire capable of carrying high currents with minimal losses.

TR4 and TR5 are mounted off-board on suitable heatsinks. Power MOSFETs, being a form of MOSFET, have very high input impedances. However, the usual anti-static precautions would seem to be unnecessary when using these components. The main risk of damage is due to unwanted high frequency oscillation, caused by the very high gain of these devices, even at quite high frequencies. The manufacturer recommends that the leads to these devices (especially the leads to the gate terminals) should be no more than 50 millimetres long. If it is essential to use longer leads, then it is recommended that a resistor of about 100 ohms or so in value is connected in series with each gate terminal, and that the resistor should be mounted close to the gate terminal. This is presumably the power MOSFET equivalent to the "base-stopper" resistors that are sometimes used to prevent instability in bipolar based circuits.

Heatsink

Judging the correct rating for a heatsink tends to be a difficult task due to the unknown and variable factors. In theory it is a straightforward task. Heatsink ratings are in degrees Centigrade per watt, and this is their thermal resistance. This is just a measure of the rise in temperature that results from each watt of power that the heatsink receives. For example, with a heatsink having a rating of 2.5 degrees Centigrade per watt, and receiving a power of 4 watts, there will be a temperature rise of 10 degrees Centigrade (2.5 degrees × 4 watts = 10 degrees).

Unfortunately, things are not quite as straightforward as simply taking the power dissipated by a transistor, and multiplying this by the rating of the heatsink in order to get the rise in temperature that will result. There is the thermal resistance of the transistor itself to take into account. Power transistors are designed to provide an efficient transfer of heat from the semiconductor chip to the case, but there is always a significant thermal resistance here. Also, there will be a certain amount

of thermal resistance between the case of the transistor an
heatsink. This should be relatively minor though, and som
silicone grease (or a synthetic substitute) can be used to ensur
a good flow of heat from one to the other. When calculatin
the temperature rise for a given dissipation figure, the therma
resistance used is the sum of these three resistances (i.e. th
transistor's rating, the heatsink's rating, and the resistanc
between the two).

In order to calculate the heatsink rating, you must firs
decide on the maximum acceptable temperature for th
transistor. Next the highest ambient temperature under whic
the device will operate must be decided. Deducting th
ambient temperature from the maximum permissible tempera
ture then gives the maximum acceptable temperature rise
Dividing this by the power dissipation then gives the minimur
acceptable overall thermal resistance. Deducting the transi
tor's thermal resistance from this, and also deducting th
transistor-to-heatsink thermal resistance, then gives the smalles
heatsink rating that will give safe operation. Note that wit
heatsink ratings the higher the figure, the less efficient th
heatsink. In other words, one having a rating of (say) 1 degre
Centigrade per watt is actually a larger and (or) more efficien
heatsink than one having a rating of 3 degrees Centigrade pe
watt. One having a rating of 1 degree Centigrade per watt
acceptable where a 1.5 degree per watt type is specified, but
1.5 degree per watt type would not be an acceptable substitut
for a 1 degree per watt heatsink.

If we take a simple example of calculating a heatsink ratin
assume that a power device must operate under the followin
conditions:-

Maximum ambient temperature	30°C
Maximum operating temperature	180°C
Maximum power dissipation	50 watts
Transistor's thermal resistance	2°C per watt
Transistor-to-heatsink resistance	0.5°C per watt

The maximum acceptable temperature rise is clearly 15
degrees (180 degrees − 30 degrees = 150 degrees). With
maximum dissipation of 50 watts, this gives an overall therma

44

resistance rating of 3 degrees Centigrade per watt (150 degrees divided by 50 watts = 3 degrees per watt). Deducting from this the thermal resistance rating of the transistor (2 degrees per watt) and the transistor-to-heatsink thermal resistance (0.5 degrees per watt) gives a rating of 0.5 degrees Centigrade per watt for the heatsink.

In practice there are a number of problems. Provided full data sheets for the power transistor can be obtained, the thermal resistance rating for the components can be ascertained (this rating is not normally to be found in short-form data). Where the thermal resistance is not quoted, it is sometimes possible to work it out anyway. For power transistors the power ("P_{TOT}") rating is usually one that assumes the transistor is mounted on a notional infinite heatsink, and is at a certain ambient temperature. Assume that the ambient temperature is the usual 25 degrees Centigrade, the transistor has a maximum operating temperature of 175 degrees Centigrade, and its power rating is 100 watts. It can take a maximum temperature rise of 150 degrees Centigrade (175 − 25 = 150), and this is produced with a power of 100 watts. The thermal resistance is therefore 1.5 degrees per watt (150 divided by 100 = 1.5).

The other figures can be difficult to define accurately. The maximum ambient temperature is something of an unknown quantity, and it is necessary to assume a fairly high figure to allow for the fact that the equipment might be used on an exceptionally hot day, or conditions that for some reason give a high ambient temperature. Also bear in mind that if the heatsink is mounted inside the case, this will result in a large rise in the temperature inside the case. This method of construction is only acceptable if the case is a type which has plenty of large ventilation holes, or large ventilation grilles. Even so, the temperature inside the case will rise quite significantly, effectively increasing the ambient temperature. I would strongly recommend mounting the power transistors and heatsinks on the exterior of the case (normally they are mounted on the rear panel). An alternative is to use a well ventilated case fitted with a cooling fan.

For the maximum temperature you could simply take the maximum temperature rating of the transistor, but this is not a good idea. Although the transistor can operate at this temperature, its reliability is unlikely to be very good at such a high temperature. Also, it leaves no safety margin if the operating conditions should ever be less favourable than expected. It is wise, where feasible, to keep the maximum designed operating temperature substantially below the maximum permissible temperature of the power transistor.

Although you might think that the maximum dissipation in the transistor is something that could be easily calculated, this is not really the case. A worse case figure can actually be calculated quite accurately for a purely resistive load, but a loudspeaker offers a load impedance that varies considerably over the audio frequency range. This renders any power dissipation calculations slightly less than accurate when a "real" load is connected to the amplifier. A reasonable safety margin therefore has to be allowed for. The thermal resistance between the heatsink and the power transistor is an unknown quantity, but it would be reasonable to assume quite a low figure here.

Obviously suitable heatsink ratings can be calculated, allowing generous safety margins where appropriate, but my advice is not to bother with this when dealing with high power audio amplifiers. Simply fit the power devices onto a very large heatsink that should be more than adequate, even if the amplifier is used under awkward conditions. I would strongly recommend the use of considerable overkill in the heatsink rating when using bipolar output transistors, where the threat of thermal runaway is an ever present one. A heatsink having a rating of about 1.2 degrees Centigrade per watt or better for each pair of output transistors should ensure safe and reliable operation with any of the amplifiers featured in this book. However, if possible use an even larger type, such as one having a rating of 1 degree Centigrade per watt or less.

Ready-made heatsinks of suitable ratings are available, and some are ready drilled to take two TO-3 power transistors such as the 2SJ49 and 2SK134. Where an amplifier has four output devices, two of these heatsinks are required. Apart from any thermal considerations, it is not physically possible to mount four TO-3 cased transistors on most heatsinks. Alternatively, all four transistors could be mounted on a single heatsink

46

aving a rating of about 0.5 degrees Centigrade per watt or
ss. If you build a bridge amplifier having eight output
evices, then you will need either four heatsinks rated at 1.2
egrees Centigrade per watt, or two rated at 0.5 degrees
entigrade per watt (and a large case to accommodate them
ll!).

nsulation

n essential point to keep in mind is that the metal TO-3
yle cases of the power MOSFETs connect internally to the
ource terminals. As the two source terminals of each com-
lementary pair are connected together anyway, this
onnection via the heatsink is of no consequence. However,
1e heatsink will then be connected to the sources of the
utput transistors, and must not be allowed to come into
lectrical contact with any other part of the circuit. Normally
1e heatsink would be mounted direct onto the metal case of
1e amplifier, which would in turn be earthed to the 0 volt
1pply rail. Either the output transistors should be insulated
rom the heatsink using standard TO-3 insulating sets, or the
eatsink must be mounted in a fashion that keeps it insulated
rom the case.

At the very least I would recommend that the output
ransistors should be insulated from the heatsink. Ideally the
eatsink should also be insulated from the case. Any break-
own in the insulation that results in the sources of the output
ransistors being connected to the earth rail could have dire
esults. This would place a short circuit on the output of the
mplifier, without any d.c. blocking as the output coupling
apacitor would be bypassed. The result of this would be a
1assive current flow until the fuse in the power supply cut off
he supply. Doubling up the insulation gives good protection
gainst this possibility.

A TO-3 insulating set consists of a thin mica or plastic
vasher plus a couple of small plastic bushes. The washer fits
etween the transistor and the heatsink. If the heatsink is not
eady-drilled for TO-3 transistors, one of these insulating
vashers can be used as a template to aid the correct position-
1g of the mounting holes. It is important that the rims of the
1ounting holes are free from any protruding pieces of metal,

which would almost certainly cut straight through the washe
and prevent it from providing the required insulation.
necessary, use a large drill bit to clean up the holes. The tw
plastic bushes fit over the mounting bolts, and prevent thes
from providing an electrical connection between the heatsin
and the transistor. One final point worth mentioning is tha
most heatsinks operate at maximum efficiency if they ar
mounted with their fins in a vertical position (not with ther
horizontally).

Supply Construction

The electrolytic capacitor in the power supply has a ver
high value, together with a fairly high voltage rating, whic
means that it is almost certain to be a single-ended type havin
tags. These are intended to be mounted on a case or chass
using a simple mounting clip. These clips are available fror
some of the larger component retailers, but it is not difficu
to improvise a suitable clip built from thin sheet aluminiun
It is probably not worth going to the trouble of building th
supply on a circuit board of any kind, although you might b
forced to do so if the smoothing capacitor is an axial type
In most cases the supply can be built using simple point-to
point wiring. Figure 3.6 gives details of the supply wirin;

This is quite straightforward, but due care should be take
when constructing the power supply unit. Apart from th
fact that the dangerous mains wiring is involved, the voltage
and currents on the output side of the supply are also quit
high. It is questionable as to whether or not 100 volts coul
give a serious shock, especially as we are talking here in term
of a d.c. supply rather than an a.c. type (which are generall
accepted as being more dangerous). You can certainly get
minor shock from a 100-volt d.c. supply though. Perhar
of greater importance, the current available from the supply :
extremely large under overload conditions. Mistakes wi
almost certainly result in some smoke and one or more of th
components in the power supply being destroyed. Be ver
careful to get the wiring right, and to avoid accidental sho
circuits. Be especially careful to connect the supply to th
amplifier with the correct polarity. This may seem to be

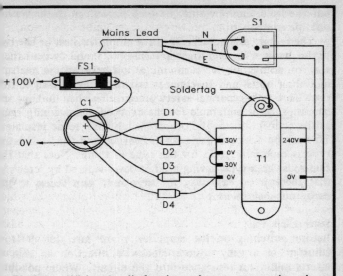

Fig.3.6   Wiring details for the mains power supply unit

trivial point, but a lot of people have made this mistake and inflicted a lot of expensive damage on their projects!

It is assumed in Figure 3.6 that the bridge rectifier is made up from four separate rectifiers. The leadouts of the rectifiers should be left fairly long (which they will probably have to be anyway), as they act like heatsinks, and help to remove heat from these components. If a ready-made bridge rectifier assembly is used, this should have " + " and " − " signs to show the two output leads and their polarity. The two leads which connect to the secondary winding of T1 will probably be marked with " ~ " symbols. With most bridge rectifiers that are designed to handle up to a few amps they must be mounted on a heatsink. The case or chassis should be more than adequate as the heatsink.

It is also assumed in Figure 3.6 that the mains transformer has twin 30-volt secondary windings connected in series to give the required 60-volt a.c. output. A twin 30-volt type is likely to prove somewhat easier to obtain than a 60-volt type,

49

but the latter can obviously be used if you can track down a
suitable component.

The metal case and chassis of the amplifier must be earthed
to the mains earth lead for safety reasons. Probably the easiest
way of doing this is to mount a soldertag on one of T1's
mounting bolts, and to connect the mains earth lead to this
tag. Observe the normal safety precautions when building the
amplifier. It is preferable for the exposed mains wiring, such
as the connections to the on/off switch (S1), to be insulated.
This can be achieved using p.v.c. sleeving, and the heat-shrink
type is especially good for this type of thing. Note that the
case must be a type having a lid or cover secured by screws so
that there is no easy way for anyone to gain access to the
dangerous mains wiring.

Setting Up

Before switching on the amplifier, make sure that VR1 is
adjusted in a fully counter-clockwise direction so that it
inserts minimum resistance into the circuit. Where possible
I would recommend trying the amplifier first with a bench
power supply. It can then be operated at a reduced supply
voltage for initial checking purposes. Somewhere in the region
of 20 to 30 volts should be sufficient to operate the circuit
properly to give a reasonable output power for testing purposes. The power supply should have current limiting that will
protect the components in the amplifier in the event that a
mistake has been made, or a component is faulty. If a suitable
power supply unit is not available, power the unit from its
mains power supply unit via a resistor of about 47 ohms in
value and having a power rating of about 10 watts. This will
provide some protection if the amplifier is faulty in some way
but it should permit it to operate at low power so that you
can ascertain whether or not it is functioning properly.

If there is any sign of a malfunction, other than reduced
output power due to the supply restrictions of course, switch
off at once and recheck the amplifier wiring, etc. If all is well
connect the unit to the mains supply unit, with no current
limiting resistor being included. It should then work quite
well, providing plenty of output power, but the distortion
performance at low volume levels will probably not be very

good. Use a multimeter set to a high d.c. current range to measure the current consumption of the unit. Temporarily removing FS1 in the power supply unit and connecting the multimeter across the fuse holder is an easy way of arranging things. With no input applied to the amplifier the current consumption should be something in the region of 10 milliamps. Adjusting VR1 in a clockwise direction should cause a steady increase in the current consumption. Advance VR1 to the point where the current reading reaches about 90 milliamps. With the multimeter removed and the fuse restored to its holder, the amplifier is ready for use.

Components

Amplifier (Fig.3.2)

Resistors (all 0.25 watt 5% carbon film)

R1	3k9
R2	10k
R3	47k
R4	68k
R5	39R
R6	15k
R7	680R
R8	1k
R9	82R
R10	1R

Potentiometer

VR1	470R sub-min hor preset

Capacitors

C1	$2\mu2$ 100V radial elect
C2	220μ 100V axial elect
C3	22μ 100V radial elect
C4	47p ceramic plate
C5	8p2 ceramic plate
C6	$4\mu7$ 63V radial elect
C7	220μ 100V radial elect
C8	2200μ 100V axial elect
C9	330n 100V polyester

Semiconductors

TR1	2SA872A
TR2	2SB716
TR3	2SD756
TR4	2SK134
TR5	2SJ49
D1	1N4148
D2	1N4148

Miscellaneous

SK1	Standard jack, or phono, etc.
SK2	Terminal post or spring terminal
SK3	Terminal post or spring terminal
	Large (1.2 degrees Centigrade per watt or better) heatsink
	Two TO-3 insulating kits
	Printed circuit board
	Wire, solder, etc.

Note that, as explained in the main text, some supply voltage and load combinations require the use of two 2SK134s in parallel for TR4, and two 2SJ49s in parallel for TR5. The 2SA872 has a lower V_{ceo} rating than the 2SA872A (90 volts as opposed to 120 volts), but it should just about be adequate in this design. The 2SA872A gives a greater safety margin, and is the better choice though. A 2SB646A is suitable for TR2, and a 2SD666A is suitable for TR3.

Power Supply (Fig.3.3)

S1	Rotary mains switch
T1	Mains primary, 60 volt secondary (refer to text for details of the required current ratings)
D1	1N5402
D2	1N5402
D3	1N5402
D4	1N5402
C1	4700μ 100V single ended electrolytic with tag connections

FS1	3A (or 3.15A) 20mm quick-blow
	20mm chassis mounting fuse holder
	Mounting clip for C1
	Wire, solder, etc.

Please read the notes in the main text regarding the power supply components before ordering the power supply components.

Op Amp Techniques

Operational amplifier techniques, with a d.c. coupled output, are often used in high power audio amplifier designs. One advantage of this method is that it avoids the need for a large (and expensive) output coupling capacitor. It can also bring advantages in terms of performance (particularly distortion at low signal levels), and makes it relatively easy to produce reliable bridge amplifier designs.

Figure 3.7 shows the basic configuration used in a power amplifier of this type. The output stage is of the usual class B complementary variety. The driver stage is a "long tailed" pair, with another long tailed pair being used as the input stage. D.C. coupling is used throughout, with the usual (for operational amplifier type circuits) dual balanced power supplies. The circuit is shown here as a non-inverting amplifier. R1 biases the input to the 0-volt supply potential, while R10 and R5 form the negative feedback loop. The input impedance of the circuit is equal to the value of R1, although with a basic operational amplifier circuit this is dependent on the value of R1 not being very high in value. The input impedance of the amplifier itself can then be ignored. The closed loop voltage gain of the circuit is equal to (R10 + R5) divided by R5.

As we shall see later, this type of circuit is easily reconfigured to operate as an inverting amplifier. This makes it easy to provide a bridge amplifier action. You simply require an inverting amplifier and a non-inverting type, with the two having feedback circuits which provide accurately matched voltage gains. With the input signal connected to the inputs of both amplifiers, and the loudspeaker connected across the non-earth outputs of the amplifiers, this gives a very good

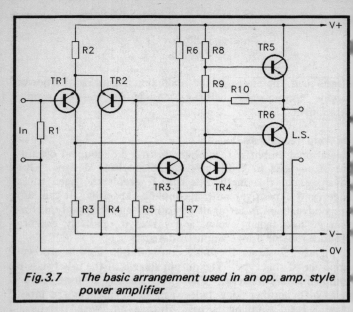

Fig.3.7   The basic arrangement used in an op. amp. style power amplifier

bridge amplifier action with no significant d.c. bias across the loudspeaker.

Op Power Amp

Figure 3.8 shows the circuit diagram for a practical power amplifier based on operational amplifier techniques. This follows the lines of the basic operational amplifier circuit discussed previously, but with some changes. Most obviously, the output transistors have been changed for power MOSFETs that enable suitably high output powers to be accommodated. A constant current generator forms the load for the driver transistor, and part of this circuit also acts as the resistive load for the other transistor in this long-tailed pair. Several resistors and capacitors are needed to ensure good stability. VR1 enables the bias current through the output stage to be trimmed to the correct figure (about 80 milliamps).

This circuit clearly has rather different supply requirements to the power amplifier featured at the beginning of this chapter. It requires supplies of plus and minus 50 volts, plus a

54

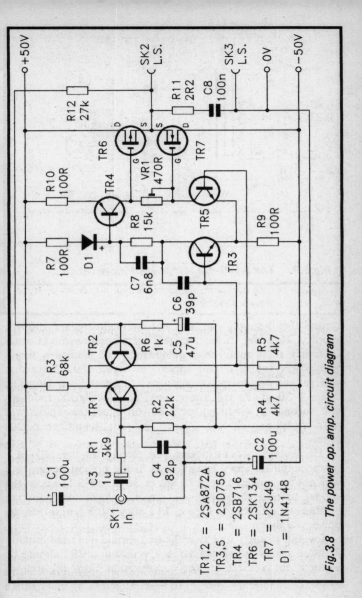

Fig.3.8   The power op. amp. circuit diagram

+50V
SK2 L.S.
SK3 L.S.
0V
−50V

R12 27k
R11 2R2
C8 100n
R10 100R
TR6
TR4
VR1 470R
TR7
TR5
R8 15k
TR3
R9 100R
R7 100R
D1
C7 6n8
C6 39p
R3 68k
TR2
R6 1k
C5 47u
R5 4k7
TR1
R2 22k
R4 4k7
C1 100u
R1 3k9
C3 1u
C4 82p
C2 100u
SK1 In

TR1,2 = 2SA872A
TR3,5 = 2SD756
TR4 = 2SB716
TR6 = 2SK134
TR7 = 2SJ49
D1 = 1N4148

55

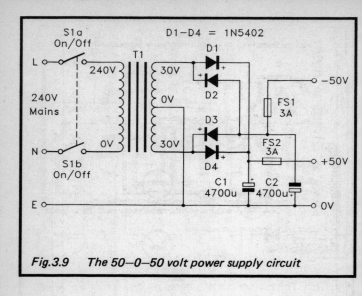

Fig.3.9   The 50—0—50 volt power supply circuit

central 0-volt supply rail, and not a straightforward 100-volt supply. However, it requires few extra components in order to satisfy these modified requirements, and a suitably modified power supply circuit appears in Figure 3.9. Note that whereas the original power supply circuit could operate using either a 30—0—30 volt transformer (or one having twin 30-volt secondary windings), or a 60-volt type, this design will only work using a 30—0—30 volt (or twin 30-volt secondary) type.

The notes on constructing and setting up the MOSFET power amplifier apply equally well to the present design, and will not be repeated here. Figures 3.10 and 3.11 show the copper pattern and component layout (respectively) for the printed circuit board. Figure 3.12 shows the wiring for the power supply unit.

I would strongly urge that the unit should be tested initially without a load connected across the output. VR1 should be adjusted for a total current consumption from the unit of about 90 milliamps, and either the positive or the negative

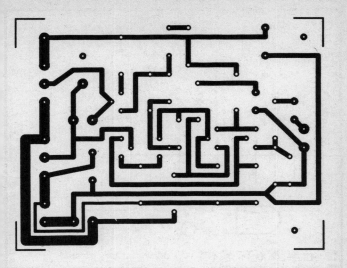

Fig.3.10   The copper track pattern for the power op. amp. unit

supply rail can be monitored. The quiescent output voltage should be within about 0.2 volts of the 0-volt supply level, and any offset here will probably be so low that it will not be possible to detect it properly with most multimeters. If there is a significant offset voltage at the output, this is indicative of a fault, and a loudspeaker should not be connected across the output until the problem has been located and corrected.

Although no fuse is shown connected in series with the output of the amplifier, I would certainly recommend adding one in the unit's non-earth output lead. A 3-amp "quick-blow" fuse should be satisfactory. Some users of high power audio amplifiers tend to look down on this practice, which does have its drawbacks. One of these is simply that there will be a small loss of power through the fuse, although this is unlikely to be large enough to be of any real significance in practice. Another problem is that the resistance of the fuse tends to reduce the damping of the amplifier on the loudspeaker.

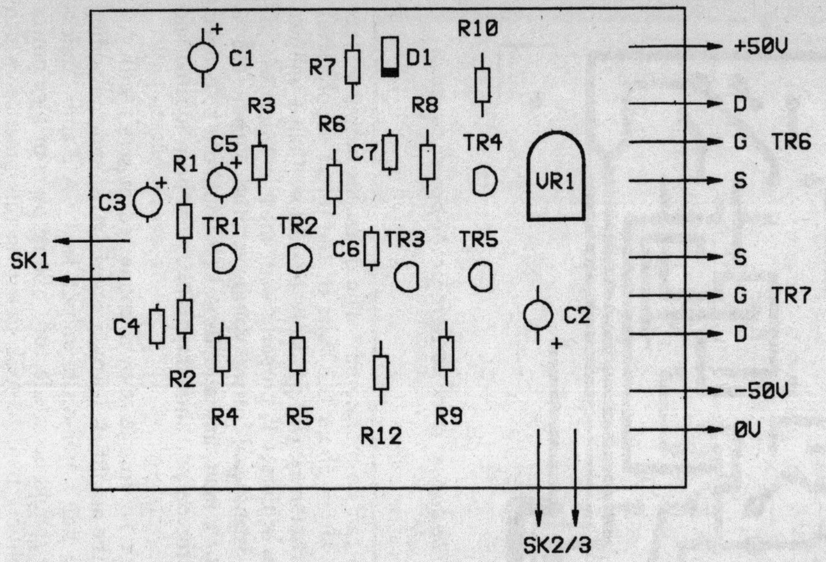

Fig.3.11   The component overlay for the p.c.b. design of Fig.3.12

58

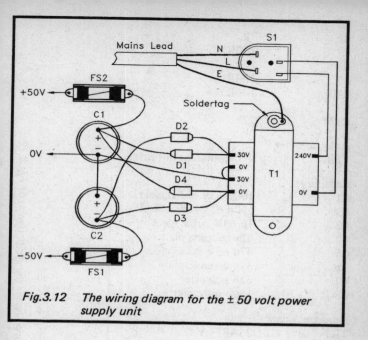

Fig. 3.12 *The wiring diagram for the ± 50 volt power supply unit*

This is undesirable, but is again something that is not likely to noticeably reduce the performance of the system. The only reason that I omitted this fuse from the prototype amplifier was because the loudspeaker system in use incorporated such a fuse. Obviously, if the loudspeaker system includes such a fuse, there is little point in including one in the amplifier.

Components

Power Op Amp (Fig.3.8)

Resistors (all 0.25 watt 5% carbon film)

R1	3k9
R2	22k
R3	68k
R4	4k7

R5	4k7
R6	1k
R7	100R
R8	15k
R9	100R
R10	100R
R11	2R2
R12	27k

Potentiometer

VR1	470R sub-min hor preset

Capacitors

C1	100μ 63V radial elect
C2	100μ 63V radial elect
C3	1μ 63V radial elect
C4	82p ceramic plate
C5	47μ 63V radial elect
C6	39p ceramic plate
C7	6n8 polyester
C8	100n polyester

Semiconductors

TR1	2SA872A
TR2	2SA872A
TR3	2SD756
TR4	2SB716
TR5	2SD756
TR6	2SK134
TR7	2SJ49
D1	1N4148

Miscellaneous

SK1	Standard jack, phono socket, etc.
SK2	Terminal post or spring terminal
SK3	Terminal post or spring terminal
	Large (1.2 degrees Centigrade per watt or better) heatsink
	Two TO-3 insulating kits
	Printed circuit board
	Wire, solder, etc.

Power Supply (Fig.3.9)

S1	Rotary mains switch
T1	Mains primary, 30–0–30 volt (or twin 30 volt) secondary (refer to text for details of the required current ratings)
D1	1N5402
D2	1N5402
D3	1N5402
D4	1N5402
C1	4700µ 63V single ended electrolytic with tag connections
C2	4700µ 63V single ended electrolytic with tag connections
FS1	3A (or 3.15A) 20mm quick-blow
FS2	3A (or 3.15A) 20mm quick-blow
	20mm chassis mounting fuse holders (2 off)
	Mounting clips for C1 and C2
	Wire, solder, etc.

Bridge Circuit

An advantage of using operational amplifier techniques in high power amplifiers is that it makes it easy to obtain a bridge amplifier for even higher output powers. The operational amplifier biasing techniques ensure that the outputs of both amplifiers are within a fraction of a volt of the 0-volt supply level, giving no significant offset voltage across the two outputs. Operational amplifier techniques also make it easy to produce amplifiers that have virtually identical voltage gains, but with one amplifier having an inverting action while the other has a non-inverting action.

The amplifier circuit of Figure 3.8 is well suited to use as one section of a bridge amplifier, and the circuit of Figure 3.13 shows a suitable amplifier circuit for the other side of the bridge. The original circuit is of the non-inverting variety, while the circuit of Figure 3.13 has been modified to give an inverting action. Apart from the change in the feedback network and input circuit to provide an inverting action, this circuit is much the same as the original. Feedback resistors R1, R11 and R12 give a voltage gain of some 28 times, which

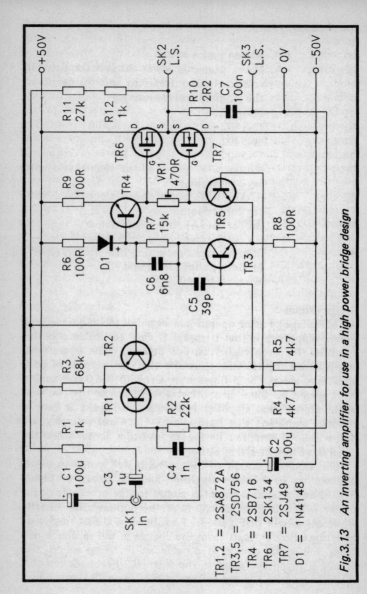

Fig.3.13 An inverting amplifier for use in a high power bridge design

TR1,2 = 2SA872A
TR3,5 = 2SD756
TR4 = 2SB716
TR6 = 2SK134
TR7 = 2SJ49
D1 = 1N4148

62

matches that of the non-inverting amplifier. The input impedance of the amplifier is only about 1k, and the input
impedance of the circuit as a whole (i.e. with both sides of
the bridge included) is somewhat lower at approximately 800
ohms. Although this is rather low, any good preamplifier
circuit should be able to handle such loading without difficulty.

The output power available from a complementary pair of
these amplifiers in a bridge configuration is quite high. The
first point that has to be made is that both amplifiers in the
bridge should have at least two pairs of power MOSFETs in
their output stages. Also, the two amplifiers should be powered from a common power supply circuit, and should not have
separate supplies. The mains transformer should have a
current rating of about 6 amps or more if really high output
powers are to be achieved. The load impedance should not be
less than 8 ohms. For good stability it is probably best to
include a C − R circuit (i.e. a 2R2 resistor in series with a
100n capacitor) from the output of each amplifier module to
the 0-volt supply. This will almost certainly be better than
using a single C − R circuit across the loudspeaker.

In theory, with one amplifier capable of delivering around
100 watts r.m.s. into an 8-ohm load, a bridge circuit with two
amplifiers should be able to deliver four times this amount.
In practice it is unlikely that these amplifiers in a bridge
arrangement will provide as much power as this. The peak
output currents are very high, giving significant voltage drops
through the output transistors. This reduces the actual maximum output power, but experiments with the prototype
equipment would suggest that powers in excess of 300 watts
r.m.s. can be readily achieved. I have not tried using more
output devices in the amplifiers in order to further boost the
output power, but it would seem reasonable to expect output
powers of up to about 400 watts r.m.s. to be achievable in
this way.

A suitable printed circuit design is shown for the inverting
amplifier module in Figures 3.14 (track pattern) and 3.15
(component overlay). Construction and setting up for this
amplifier module follow closely along the same lines as those
for the non-inverting version of the amplifier, and they will
not be described again here.

63

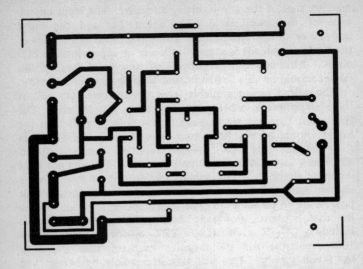

Fig.3.14   The track pattern for the inverting MOSFET power amplifier

Components Inverting Op Power Amp (Fig.3.13)

Resistors (all 0.25 watt 5% carbon)

R1	1k
R2	22k
R3	68k
R4	4k7
R5	4k7
R6	100R
R7	15k
R8	100R
R9	100R
R10	2R2
R11	27k
R12	1k

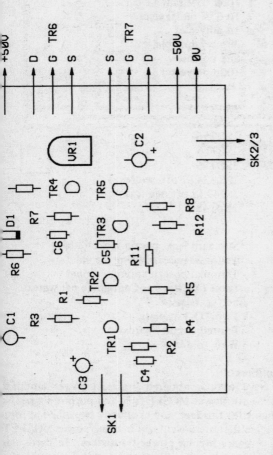

Fig.3.15   The component overlay for the printed circuit design of Fig.3.14

65

Potentiometer
VR1   470R sub-min hor preset

Capacitors
C1   100µ 63V radial elect
C2   100µ 63V radial elect
C3   1µ 63V radial elect
C4   1n polyester
C5   39p ceramic plate
C6   6n8 polyester
C7   100n polyester

Semiconductors
TR1   2SA872A
TR2   2SA872A
TR3   2SD756
TR4   2SB716
TR5   2SD756
TR6   2SK134 (2 off, see text)
TR7   2SJ49 (2 off, see text)
D1   1N4148

Miscellaneous
SK1   Standard jack, phono socket, etc.
SK2   Terminal post or spring terminal
SK3   Terminal post or spring terminal
                   Large (1.2 degrees Centigrade per watt or
                   better) heatsink
                   Two TO-3 insulating kits
                   Printed circuit board
                   Wire, solder, etc.

Bipolar Amplifiers
So far we have only considered practical power amplifier
designs which have power MOSFETs in the output stage. No
apology is made for this fact, and as already explained at some
length, there are definite advantages in using power MOSFETs
rather than ordinary bipolar power transistors. In particular,
the lack of any problems with thermal stabilisation makes
power MOSFETs a good choice for home constructed power
amplifier designs.

However, for those who prefer to use bipolar transistors throughout, two bipolar transistor high power circuits are provided here. These are basically just the operational amplifier style inverting and non-inverting circuits described previously, but modified to take bipolar transistors in the output stages. The circuit diagrams for these two amplifiers are provided in Figure 3.16 (non-inverting amplifier) and Figure 3.17 (inverting amplifier).

The first point to note is that it is not possible to simply replace each power MOSFET with a bipolar power transistor. The current gain of a typical power transistor is only about 50, which is nothing like high enough with a collector current of only about 8 milliamps or so in the driver stage. Either the current flow in the driver stage must be considerably increased, or extra transistors must be used in the output stage in order to boost its current gain. In this case the driver current is left unaltered, and two Darlington pairs are used in the output stage. In fact the second transistor in each Darlington pair is a pair of parallel connected power transistors, complete with emitter resistors. This enables high output currents and powers to be handled more safely, particularly if the amplifiers are used in a bridge configuration.

The choice of output transistors is important in this application, where high frequency performance can suffer if a poor choice is made. Transistors such as the 2N3055, MJE2955, 2N3773, 2N6609, etc., are often used as the output transistors in high power audio amplifiers. In some ways they are less than ideal for this application though. In the case of the 2N3055 and its complements, it should be borne in mind that its V_{ceo} rating is only 60 volts, although it often seems to be used in audio power designs operating with supply voltages as high as 100 volts (or dual balanced 50-volt supplies). When subjected to maximum voltage the device is likely to have a reverse bias, which makes this practice less risky than it might appear, although it is still one that I would not recommend.

Another problem with many high power transistors is that they have cut-off frequencies of only about 200kHz or so. While this may seem to be adequate for devices that will be used for audio amplification, with an upper frequency limit

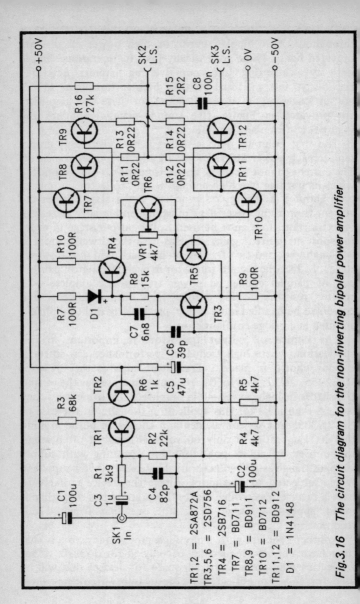

Fig.3.16 The circuit diagram for the non-inverting bipolar power amplifier

TR1,2 = 2SA872A
TR3,5,6 = 2SD756
TR4 = 2SB716
TR7 = BD711
TR8,9 = BD911
TR10 = BD712
TR11,12 = BD912
D1 = 1N4148

68

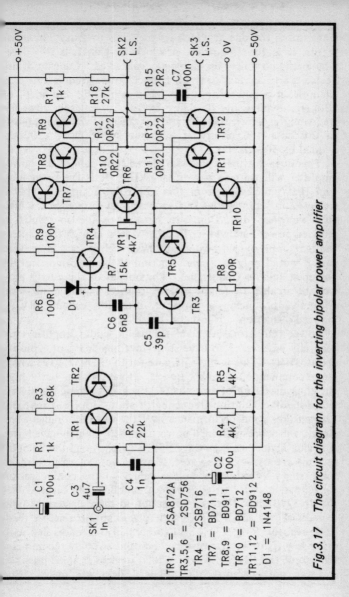

Fig.3.17 The circuit diagram for the inverting bipolar power amplifier

TR1,2 = 2SA872A
TR3,5,6 = 2SD756
TR4 = 2SB716
TR7 = BD711
TR8,9 = BD911
TR10 = BD712
TR11,12 = BD912
D1 = 1N4148

69

of 20kHz, it has to be remembered that the F_t figure for a transistor is the one at which its gain falls to unity. In other words, it is the frequency at which its gain falls to a level where it is no longer providing any gain at all. The gain of the device starts to fall away at a much lower frequency. For example, if a power transistor has a gain of 50 and an F_t of 200kHz, dividing the F_t figure by the current gain gives the frequency at which the gain of the transistor starts to roll-off. In this case it is clearly at a frequency of 4kHz (200kHz divided by 50 = 4kHz).

This does not mean that the closed loop gain of the power amplifier will start to roll-off at 4kHz. It is the open loop gain that will suffer from this low roll-off figure. This is reflected in less negative feedback at high frequencies, which gives increased distortion. In most cases it also results in reduced power bandwidth. In other words, at high frequencies the maximum output power falls away slightly, and in a severe case it would only be a small fraction of the maximum output power at middle frequencies. The output of the circuit may well be unable to follow sudden changes in the input level correctly, producing a form of distortion called "slewing induced distortion", or just "SID".

Power transistors intended for use in audio amplifiers are generally engineered to have somewhat higher F_ts of typically about 3MHz. This is the F_t figure for the BD911/912s which are recommended for this design. Even with a fairly high current gain figure of around 100, the gain of these transistors will not roll-off until a frequency of about 30kHz is reached. This ensures good performance over the full audio range. The circuit will work with high power transistors which have lower F_ts, and devices such as the 2N3773 (n.p.n.) and the 2N6609 (p.n.p.) are usable. However, it might be necessary to make some slight adjustments to the values of the compensation capacitors in order to ensure good stability. In order to get the 2N3773 and 2N6609 to function in these designs I found it necessary to add a 33p ceramic plate capacitor across feedback resistor R16. This will presumably be necessary with other low F_t power transistors. I would strongly recommend the use of the BD911/912 or similar devices if at all possible, and can not guarantee that other devices will prove to be entirely satisfactory in this design.

Thermal Stability

Using bipolar output transistors means that there is a problem with thermal stability to overcome. This design uses the standard method, which is to have a transistor in the amplified diode configuration to control the quiescent output bias current. This is based on TR6, and has its output voltage (and hence the quiescent bias current) controlled by VR1. VR1 should be set so that the output bias current is about 110 milliamps, which equates to about 100 milliamps through the output transistors.

Of course, TR6 should be mounted on the heatsink which takes TR8, TR9, TR11 and TR12, so that it responds to their rise in temperature, and stabilises the output bias current. The output current should be monitored to ensure that it does not rise significantly as the output transistors heat up. If necessary, a better thermal contact between TR6 and the output transistors must be obtained in order to prevent a continual rise in the output current. Alternatively, readjusting VR1 to return the current drain to about 110 milliamps might give satisfactory results. Note though, that this method will give a low bias current (and possibly high cross-over distortion) each time the amplifier is used, before the output transistors become heated up. Also, it does not absolutely guarantee that thermal runaway will not occur. It is possible that the quiescent current might drop slightly as the output transistors heat up. This would suggest a thermal coupling that is too good, and the coupling to TR6 should then be loosened slightly.

No construction details are provided for these two amplifiers, but they can be constructed along much the same lines as the power MOSFET designs. It would probably be possible to use the same printed circuit designs after a small amount of modification. I tested the prototype amplifiers using the power MOSFET circuit boards plus some hard wiring. This did not give particularly neat finished results, but the amplifiers worked well enough.

Remember that TR7 and TR10 require heatsinks. They can be mounted on the same heatsink as the output transistors if desired, or they can be fitted on their own heatsink (one of about 3 degrees Centigrade per watt should suffice). Bear in mind that the metal tabs of the BD711/712/911/912 transistors connect internally to their collector terminals. It is essential that all these devices should be properly insulated from their heatsinks using TO-220 insulating kits. These consist of a single insulating washer plus one plastic bush (just one bush, since this type of transistor has only one mounting bolt).

These amplifiers produce output powers that are comparable to the power MOSFET circuits, and if anything, they will produce what are generally slightly higher output powers for a given set of operating conditions. I have not made any distortion measurements on the bipolar versions of the amplifiers, and in this respect I would not expect them to be as good as the power MOSFET designs. However, listening tests would suggest that they have quite a reasonable level of performance in this respect, and they should certainly give adequate for most high power audio applications.

Components

Non-inverting Bipolar Power Amplifier (Fig.3.16)

Resistors (0.25 watt 5% carbon unless indicated)

R1	3k9
R2	22k
R3	68k
R4	4k7
R5	4k7
R6	1k
R7	100R
R8	15k
R9	100R
R10	100R
R11	OR22 3 watt
R12	OR22 3 watt
R13	OR22 3 watt
R14	OR22 3 watt
R15	2R2
R16	27k

Potentiometer
VR1   4k7 sub-min hor preset

Capacitors
C1	100μ 63V radial elect
C2	100μ 63V radial elect
C3	1μ 63V radial elect
C4	82p ceramic plate
C5	47μ 63V radial elect
C6	39p ceramic plate
C7	6n8 polyester
C8	100n polyester

Semiconductors
TR1	2SA872A
TR2	2SA872A
TR3	2SD756
TR4	2SB716
TR5	2SD756
TR6	2SD756
TR7	BD711
TR8	BD911
TR9	BD911
TR10	BD712
TR11	BD912
TR12	BD912
D1	1N4148

Miscellaneous
SK1	Standard jack, phono socket, etc.
SK2	Terminal post or spring terminal
SK3	Terminal post or spring terminal
	Large (1.2 degrees Centigrade per watt or better) heatsink
	Six TO-220 insulating kits
	Printed circuit board
	Wire, solder, etc.

Inverting Bipolar Power Amplifier (Fig.3.17)

Resistors (0.25 watt 5% carbon unless indicated)

R1	1k
R2	22k
R3	68k
R4	4k7
R5	4k7
R6	100R
R7	15k
R8	100R
R9	100R
R10	OR22 3 watt
R11	OR22 3 watt
R12	OR22 3 watt
R13	OR22 3 watt
R14	1k
R15	2R2
R16	27k

Potentiometer

VR1	4k7 sub-min hor preset

Capacitors

C1	100μ 63V radial elect
C2	100μ 63V radial elect
C3	4μ7 63V radial elect
C4	1n polyester
C5	39p ceramic plate
C6	6n8 polyester
C7	100n polyester

Semiconductors

TR1	2SA872A
TR2	2SA872A
TR3	2SD756
TR4	2SB716
TR5	2SD756
TR6	2SD756
TR7	BD711

TR8	BD911
TR9	BD911
TR10	BD712
TR11	BD912
TR12	BD912
D1	1N4148

Miscellaneous

SK1	Standard jack, phono socket, etc.
SK2	Terminal post or spring terminal
SK3	Terminal post or spring terminal
	Large (1.2 degrees Centigrade per watt or better) heatsink
	Six TO-220 insulating kits
	Printed circuit board
	Wire, solder, etc.

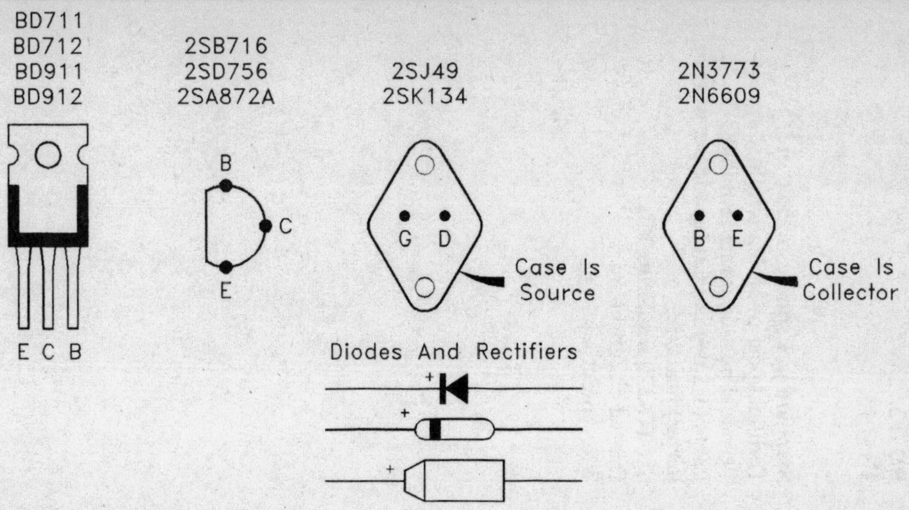

BD711
BD712
BD911
BD912

E C B

2SB716
2SD756
2SA872A

B C E

2SJ49
2SK134

G D

Case Is Source

Diodes And Rectifiers

2N3773
2N6609

B E

Case Is Collector

Fig.3.18 Semiconductor pinout details (transistors are all viewed from underside)

76

Notes

Notes

Please note overleaf is a list of other titles that are available in our range of Radio, Electronics and Computer Books.

These should be available from all good Booksellers, Radio Component Dealers and Mail Order Companies.

However, should you experience difficulty in obtaining any title in your area, then please write directly to the Publisher enclosing payment to cover the cost of the book plus adequate postage.

If you would like a complete catalogue of our entire range of Radio, Electronics and Computer Books then please send a Stamped Addressed Envelope to:

BERNARD BABANI (publishing) LTD
THE GRAMPIANS
SHEPHERDS BUSH ROAD
LONDON W6 7NF
ENGLAND